Strategic Reading on Latin America, 3rd Ed.

A compilation of previously published articles.

by

Russell W. Ramsey, Ph.D., D.Min.

ISBN: 0-75962-731-2

This book is printed on acid free paper.

1stBooks – rev. 9/12/01

TABLE OF CONTENTS

This third edition is dedicated to the late COL John J. Madigan, III, US Army, Retired. As editor of <u>Parameters,</u> he conceived a series of articles and authorized an extract version. He was a beloved and great soldier, strategist, and scholar. Additional book reviews on Latin American strategic issues are included from other publications for the first time in an effort to be comprehensive.

Since their appearance in <u>Parameters,</u> the following errata are noted and corrected by the author:

1. "National Security Agency" should read "Central Intelligence Agency." P. 20, line 37
2. Professor I. L. Horowitz' book here reviewed was an incomplete draft form. The final version contained vital new material. P. 22, line 7-9
3. Europa Publications has no official connection with the (British) <u>Army Quarterly & Defence Journal</u>. This correction in no way affects nor diminishes the author's high opinion of both publications. P. 30; line 2-3
4. The Latin American volume in this series, starting in 1997, is written by Robert T. Buckman, who continues the standard of excellence shown by Pierre D. Dostert. P. 35, line 24-6
5. While some of the writers are affiliated with the CSIS, the book is not a CSIS product as stated. p. 35, Line 30-1; p. 35; line 1-3

Russell W. Ramsey Ph.D, D. Min.

3d Edition edited by: Patricia J. Frobe

January 2001

Strategic Reading on Latin America
<u>Parameters</u> Summer 1994
RUSSELL W. RAMSEY

Latin America emerges in the 1990s as the post-Cold War world's humane region, exciting in the present and headed for a promising future. While some observers remain pessimistic, a parcel of well-written recent books brings the reader into the geostrategic vitality of Latin America on a positive note.

Pierre Etienne Dostert's *Latin America 1993* is the 27th edition of the Stryker-Post series on the world's regions. Dostert has unusual credentials. Judge, economist, Africa analyst, and master of four languages, he offers credible descriptions of the conflict zones, country by country, between economic privatization and booming democratization. Complementing this book topically and philosophically are the February and March 1993 issues of *Current History*, edited by William W. Finan, Jr. The February issue highlights Mexico and NAFTA from many viewpoints, and the March number has balanced contents on national security issues such as the Andean narcotics war, Panama's continuing instability, and Brazil's battle to privatize the economy. In 1994, only the March issue is dedicated to Latin America, and the analysis is more pessimistic.

Some analysts consider Latin America's present wave of privatization and democratization to be skin deep. There is historical precedent for this skepticism. Generals Simon Bolivar and Jose Francisco San Martin, principal military architects of the long independence campaigns against Spain in the 1820s, spoke ardently of a region searching for a constitutional order and free-market economies. San Martin said that his mission as soldier-liberator was "to protect the innocent oppressed, to help the unfortunate, to restore their rights to the inhabitants of this region, and to promote their happiness." [1820, quoted by Henry Brackenridge] In their later years, both San Martin and Bolivar lamented their betrayed dreams when *caudillos*—a genre of quasi-military, semi-feudal chieftains—emerged instead of democratically elected presidents.

At the dawn of the 20th century, positivist economic and social policies led by strongmen figures again seemed to derail the democratic impulse. US influence during the high age of maritime imperialism, 1898-1932, imparted both modernization and reinforcement for opportunistic strongmen in Central America and the Caribbean. Cold War era democratic impulses were sometimes artificially focused in Latin America into choices between leftist or anti-communist administrations as the USSR and Cuba challenged the West and threatened to install totalitarian systems. Economic policy in the era took its cues from Raul Prebisch's structuralism, a form of an inefficient economic nationalism that many US analysts wrongly thought to be a preference for socialism.

So it comes as no surprise that academic analysts are hesitant to proclaim deeply institutionalized democracy and effective free enterprise systems in Latin America at Cold War's end. Two books sum up well the entire pattern of revolutionary challenges which occurred during the years of East-West conflict.

Professors Michale Radu and Vladimir Tismaneanu, both Romanian exiles to the United States, produced *Latin American Revolutionaries: Groups, Goals, Methods* in 1990, showing that much of Latin America's highly publicized romance with armed revolutionists during the Cold War was often an inauthentic carbon copy of European radicalism. Professor Timothy P. Wickham-Crowley, in his 1992 *Guerrillas and Revolution in Latin America: A Comparative Study of Insurgents and Regimes Since 1956*, explains with convincing methodology why it is that revolutionary movements succeeded only in Cuba and Nicaragua. Given that Latin America is the world's least militarized region, since 1830, measured as percent of gross national product expended on arms, soldiers per thousand citizens, and percentage of deaths in armed conflict, Professor Wickham-Crowley's thesis—that Latin America's other guerrilla forces never really had serious legitimacy—is consistent and credible.

Professor Abraham Lowenthal's *Partners in Conflict*, written at the height of the Contra-Sandinista war in Nicaragua and the government-FMLN war in El Salvador, was the first major political analysis on the region to identify the positive trends seen in the 1990s. One can see US policy initiatives that follow Lowenthal's blueprint to encourage political and economic integration and discourage externally imposed conflict. Excellent description of democratization in progress is found in Robert A. Pastor's *Whirlpool: U.S. Foreign Policy toward Latin America and the Caribbean*, 1992. Professor Pastor was a policy adviser to President Jimmy Carter and has remained at the Carter Center of Emory University in Atlanta, working with the peripatetic former President in the supervision of controversial elections in Latin America. Panama, Mexico, Puerto Rico, and the Organization of American States receive strong and unique treatment in this book which is both an analysis and a testimony.

While there is a spate of journal articles on specific economic issues within Latin America, there is not a single book which fully describes the complete economic process, the dimension which most analysts hold central to the survival of democratization. Professor John Williamson edited a collection of essays in 1990 published as *Latin American Adjustment: How Much Has Really Happened?*, a cautionary note to the fact that much privatization moves at snail's pace. More optimistic is Michael Novak's *This Hemisphere of Liberty*, also published in 1990. Novak is a Catholic theologian and economist who has found liberation theology to be of exaggerated importance. He shows the cultural shock of converting Indo-Hispanic Latin America to modern neo-liberal economics. Robert Devlin in his 1992 *Debt and Crisis in Latin America: The Supply Side of the Story* was responding to demands for an explanation of runaway public indebtedness in the region during the 1980s. His study calls into question the assumption that private banking policy helps the privatization process. There is a great need for a book on the family of regional treaties carried out under the principles of the General Agreement on Tariff and Trade (GATT): NAFTA, MERCOSUR (the South American cone), Andean Common Market, Central American Common Market, and CARICOM (the Caribbean). Many national security issues arise from these accords.

US scholars often have not discerned that the age of gunboat diplomacy, say from 1898 to 1932, and the Cold War, 1947 to 1989, were two different phenomena. A paradigm of convenience and doubtful intellectual merit was created according to which US Cold War policy in Latin America was a pretense for continuing the old policies of gunboat diplomacy among conveniently authoritarian governments. Latin America was presented as a heavily militarized region that would overthrow most of its own governments if the United States had not strengthened indigenous militarism. The new crop of books on national security topics is more eclectic and covers more topics.

Professor G. Pope Atkins has edited *South America into the 1990s: Evolving International Relationships in a New Era.* This set of essays appeared in 1990 as General Augusto Pinochet was turning over authority to legally elected civilians in Chile, as Paraguay was moving toward its first democratic administration in decades, and as Argentina was modifying its constitution to limit the use of the army to defense against foreign invasion. It shows internal South American security dimensions previously not understood by the national security community. Professor Jonathan Hartlyn edited *The United Sates and Latin American Relations in the 1990s: Beyond the Inter-American System*, a 1993 volume available in both hard cover and paperback. Two essays on the economic systems rapidly evolving in the region are among the best available. The political essays focus on the outer ends of the political spectrum and neglect the emerging consensus majority in several countries. The essays on the role of the Latin American military forces reflect a change in regional events as well as in author viewpoints. These analysts in the 1980s saw Latin America's own armed forces as a greater threat to democracy than the Soviet-Cuban subversion machine. Today, they visualize limited roles for the air and naval forces but find little use for armies in the region. A shorter, more balanced book on national security issues in the region is *Evolving U.S. Strategy for Latin America and the Caribbean*, essays edited by Professor L. Erik Kjonnerod. Delicate questions about relative US and Latin American military responsibilities for the drug war are carefully stated. Sub-regional assessments address the visible security threats.

During the peak years of the Cold War, the United States dedicated about two percent of its security assistance money and four percent of its official arms sales and transfers to the entire Latin American region. Despite the ugly misbehavior of several uniformed regimes, military professionalism flourished in Latin America during the era, and a cordial network of useful relationships was forged between US and Latin American officers. Today, such questions as the future of US-Latin American military relations and roles revolve around the continuance of the roundtable, and the maintenance of a seat at the table for all the knights. This concept is institutionally expressed in the Inter-American Defense Board, the military advisory arm of the Organization of American States, and was explained well by Anthony Harrigan in his article "Inter-American Defense in the Seventies" (*Military Review*, April 1970). The Kjonnerod volume is singular among the recent wave of books on Latin American security topics by making anew the case for the roundtable. Some of it was visible in August 1993 when the US Army School of the Americas assembled academics, diplomats, and military officials at the 5th Latin American Conference to discuss the military role in the privatization and democratization process.

In the November 1993 issue of *Hispanic American Historical Review* there appears an essay by Professor Benjamin Keen on the huge contribution made to the study of Latin America by the late Professor Lewis Hanke. The acknowledged dean of Latin American history in the United States, Hanke discovered the humane origins of Latin American society, presenting the struggle waged by the priest Bartolomeo de las Casas to obtain justice for the Indians under the Spanish Empire. In the wake of las Casas' writings came the Black Legend, convenient to British Protestants who wanted a moral basis to wage mayhem against Spain's gold and silver fleets on the high seas. Black Legend proponents like Oliver Cromwell painted all Hispanic men-at-arms as savage cowards, morally incapable of soldierly behavior; neo-liberals and leftists in the US academic community reinvented this convenient paradigm during the Cold War, which is now over. One suspects that Professor Hanke would counsel an end to the vendetta.

The Western Hemisphere has the world's most cordial military-to-military relationships and the fewest wars. Nuclear arms are rejected in Latin America, as are chemical and biological weapons, the irresponsible use of mines, and the practice of coup d'etat. Latin American men-at-arms wear blue helmets for the United Nations in worldwide hot spots and uphold human rights at home and abroad. Yet the drug war, several Indian uprisings, Fidel Castro's eventual demise, the complete demilitarization of the Sandinistas and the Contras in Nicaragua, and the future of the Panama Canal all present national security questions. The books mentioned herein provide interesting and professionally solid reading.

BIBLIOGRAPHY

G. Pope Atkins, ed., *South America into the 1990s: Evolving International Relationships in a New Era* (Boulder, Colo: Westview Press, 1990).

Robert Devlin, *Debt and Crisis in Latin America: The Supply Side of the Story* (Princeton, J.J.: Princeton Univ. Press, 1992).

Pierre Etienne Dostert, *Latin America 1993* (27th ed.; Washington: Stryker-Post Publications, 1993).

Georges Fauriol, ed., *Security in the Americas* (Washington: National Defense Univ. Press, 1989).

William W. Finan, Jr., ed., *Current History*, "Mexico," February 1993; "Latin America," March 1993; and "Latin America," March 1994.

Jonathan Hartlyn, et al., ed., *The United States and Latin American Relations in the 1990s: Beyond the Inter-American System* (Chapel Hill: Univ. of North Carolina Press, 1993).

Anthony Harrigan, "Inter-American Defense in the Seventies," *Military Review*, 50 (April 1970), 3-9.

L. Erik Kjonnerod, *Evolving U.S. Strategy for Latin America and the Caribbean* (Washington: National Defense Univ. Press, 1992).

Abraham Lowenthal, *Partners in Conflict* (Baltimore: Johns Hopkins Univ. Press, 1987).

Michael Novak, *This Hemisphere of Liberty* (New York: Paulist Press, 1990).

Robert A. Pastor, *Whirlpool: U.S. Foreign Policy Toward Latin America and the Caribbean* (Princeton, J.J.: Princeton Univ. Press, 1992).

Michale Radu and Vladimir Tismaneanu, *Latin American Revolutionaries: Groups, Goals, Methods*, Foreign Policy Institute Book (Washington: Pergamon Brassey, 1990).

Russell W. Ramsey, "The Role of Latin American Armed Forces in the 1990s," *Strategic Review* (Fall 1992), reprinted in *Proceedings, 5th Latin American Conference* (Ft. Benning, Ga.: US Army School of the Americas, 1993).

Lars Schoultz, *National Security and United States Policy towards America: A Comparative Study of Insurgents and Regimes Since 1956* (Princeton, N.J.: Princeton Univ. Press, 1992).

John Williamson, ed., *Latin American Adjustment: How Much Has Really Happened?* (Washington: Washington Inst. For International Economics, 1990).

The Reviewer: Lieutenant Colonel Russell W. Ramsey (USAR, Ret.) is Distinguished Resident Professor, US Army School of the Americas, Ft.

Benning, Georgia. He is a graduate of the US Military Academy and holds a Ph.D. from the University of Florida. His *Soldiers and Guerrillas* (Bogota, 1961, and 2d ed., 2000), published in Spanish, is the standard history of the rural violence in Columbia.

US Strategy for Latin America
<u>Parameters</u> Autumn 1994
RUSSELL W. RAMSEY

"My mission is to protect the innocent oppressed, to help the unfortunate, to restore their rights to the inhabitants of this region, and to promote their happiness," wrote General Jose Francisco de San Martin, the military architect of independence for southern South America, on 8 September 1820.[1] General Simon Bolivar, the emancipator of northern South America, opined in 1826, "The man of honor has no country save that in which the citizen's rights are protected and the sacred character of humanity is respected."[2] Colombia's first President, the lawyer-General Francisco de Paula Santander, stated repeatedly in the 1820s that "arms have given us independence; laws will give us freedom" as he established the principle of civilian control over the armed forces.[3]

Yet Bolivar himself expressed anguish over the apparent triumph of *caudillismo*—rule by para-military strongmen—that frustrated constitutional democracy in several Latin American countries for a century. The movement to professionalization of Latin America's small armed forces, after 1880, included a tendency during the Cold War years for military leaders in several countries to exert an extra-constitutional praetorian role.[4] At various points in the Cold War, military and police forces in a dozen Latin American countries carried out human rights abuses under the guise of national security. Marxist-Leninist regimes in Nicaragua and Cuba engaged in massive increased in troops and armaments, achieving force levels not previously seen in the region.

Redeeming the Dream

Latin America's armed forces now emerge at the end of the Cold War as a positive force amid bold democratization and economic development within the world's oldest and largest homogeneous block of constitutional and independent nation-states. Measured since 1830 by percent of the gross domestic product spent on the armed forces, percent of the national manpower in military uniform, number of wars, relative levels of armaments, and percent of citizens killed or displaced by war, Latin America is also the world's least bellicose and least militarized region.[5]

Military praetorianism under all banners is today in disrepute, and the posse comitatus principle is now the law throughout Latin America except in Haiti and Cuba.[6] There are 12 Latin American military contingents serving in the 26 international peacekeeping forces operational in 1994.[7] Shared linguistic, training, and operations experiences between US and Latin American military officers today contribute to democratically obedient armed forces relationships.[8] Finally, a case can be made that Latin America's armed forces, since 1961, are among the world's regional leaders in low-cost civic action programs that improve the quality of life for remote populations and help the general public in times of civil disaster.[9]

The Core of a US Policy

US military policy for Latin America in the 1990s, and into the 21st century, calls for quiet, inexpensive steps through which to institutionalize and strengthen the functional linkage among the Western Hemisphere's military leaders. The strategic applications all flow from that policy, save in the cases of Cuba, Nicaragua, Haiti, and Panama, whose military and public security officers are estranged from their US counterparts for differing historical reasons. A renewal of the once cordial military-to-military relations with these four nations is attainable during the remaining years of the 1990s.

The possible strategies emanating from this *hermandad* (translated as "brotherhood" without gender, the name for a defensive municipal structure in Medieval Spain) hold bright hopes for regional peace. With a tiny per capita regional investment of national security funds, this "brotherhood of the Americas" can be an exportable model by which to secure democratic liberties and open-market economic success in a climate free of international wars, unilateral military interventions, class revolutions, ethnic and religious conflict, and organized crime.

Much analytical literature on Latin America stresses the praetorian and abusive nature of its armed forces. US national security programs during the Cold War era often are blamed for having fostered both tendencies. Yet one analyst concluded in a multi-regional analysis that the United States had little leverage through which to force behavioral change. Careful analysis of these US programs in Latin America reveals that they rarely exceeded two percent of all security assistance allocations and four percent of authorized foreign military sales carried out worldwide during the period. The programs had little effect on armed revolutions led by the military.[10]

Current US security assistance programs in the region barely total one-half billion dollars annually, most of which is concentrated in closing out the Central American conflicts in the 1980s, and in the Andean counternarcotics campaign, two areas where the United States bears indisputable moral responsibility to assist.[11] The total cost of continuing the policy of cordial, constructive US-Latin American military-to-military relations would remain a tiny fraction of the US national defense budget. If this sum could be divided into the total strategic value of the region,[12] the ensuing ratio would reveal a highly cost-effective defense policy.

Lieutenant Colonel Russell W. Ramsey, USAR Ret., is Distinguished Resident Professor, US Army School of the Americas, Ft. Benning, Georgia. He received a B.S. from the US Military Academy, an M.A. from the University of Southern Mississippi, and a Ph.D. from the University of Florida, and he is a graduate of the US Army Command and General Staff College. He was a teacher and the pilot project officer who set up counterinsurgency training at the School of the Americas in 1961 and has lectured and published extensively on Latin American security issues. His *Soldiers and Guerrillas* (Bogota, 1981, and 2d ed., 2000), published in Spanish, is the standard history of the rural violence in Columbia.

A Permanent Military Dialogue

The first item on the strategy agenda is to build an institutionalized future for the continued relationship. The Organization of American States is the world's oldest regional assembly. The Inter-American Defense Board (IADB), a military advisory body, has only a consultative relationship with the OAS. There is much preoccupation in Western Hemispheric political circles about militarism within Latin America and about armed interventionism by the United States in Latin America. While a factual case can be made that these concerns are outdated by events, the future of the IADB is under debate. Some see it as a positive vehicle for international peacekeeping operations, while to others it is warmed-over Cold War baggage.[13]

The United States is only one actor on the stage. Clearly, the era of gunboat diplomacy (1870-1933) and the era of Cold War preemptive interventionism (1947-1989) are over; Uncle Sam neither can nor should attempt to force a regional security regime upon nations which reject the structure. But to the extent that quiet diplomacy can prevail, the United States should work actively to preserve and enrich the existing Western Hemispheric security policy and structure.

Under the Carter-Torrijos Treaties ratified in 1979, US Southern Command (SOUTHCOM) in Panama must depart or have its presence renegotiated prior to the last day of 1999. A useful US policy, therefore, would be to work for the creation of a regional structure that provides focused national security planning for the United Sates in a cooperative hemispheric security setting. A US Western

Hemisphere Command (WHC) should be created to replace SOUTHCOM, and an OAS Security Commission, an enhanced version of the IADB, should be created by amending the OAS Charter. The WHC would be structurally located within the newly empowered OAS Security Commission, whose geographic headquarters should be in a convenient, neutral, and uncontested location. Five sub-regional planning elements of this proposed OAS Security Commission would structurally parallel the current family of trade pacts organized under the General Agreement on Tariff and Trade (GATT).[14]

Thus, the North American Region would manage security planning for the North American Free Trade Alliance (NAFTA) countries (Canada, the United States, and Mexico); the Caribbean Region would do the same task for the Caribbean Common Market and Caribbean Free Trade Agreement countries (CARICOM/CAFTA); the Central American Region for the Central American Common Market nations; the Andean Region for the Andean Regional Free Trade Pact countries; and the Southern Cone Region for this sub-region's trade pact members (called MERCOSUR, by the Spanish acronym). The creation of a small, sub-regional headquarters for each of these elements would help to reduce fears of a "military monolith" on Latin American soil.

Any successful national security system depends upon the balanced triad of political, economic, and military objectives and policies. Discussions of future US-Latin American relations call for the fostering of cordial, consultative relationships in the political sphere, a goal quite achievable given the excellent quality of US State Department career service diplomats who worked in Latin America during the last decade of the Cold War. The economic dimension of the triad may be more difficult to achieve. Economic power is clustered in bewildering arrays of multinational corporations, governmental agencies, regional trade treaty boards, national companies with private and public ownership, and, to be sure, powerful extra-hemispheric interests which neither parallel nor own allegiance to the political structures in the region.[15] Nevertheless, the emergence of a subculture of economic superstars in a dozen Latin American countries in the past decade suggests that a consultative hemispheric network in the economic sphere is already taking form and will not lack for competent personnel.[16]

The Possible Strategy Agenda

With the political, economic, and military spheres of the Western Hemisphere moving toward structural collegiality, the military strategies for maintaining peace and defense at minimum cost are workable. The military and law enforcement strategy agenda for the remaining years of the 20th century and the early 21st century contains ten objectives. These are:

- maintain and improve the hemispheric national security framework, with seats at the roundtable for every country
- bolster military professionalism
- reduce the power of the region's drug cartels
- cope humanely with mass migration
- increase Latin American participation in protection of air and sea lanes of communication, with special emphasis on the Panama Canal
- foster the blue-helmet and civic action capabilities of Latin America's armed forces
- institutionalize the protection of human rights by the armed forces
- maintain a regional defense philosophy which opposes the use of nuclear, chemical, biological, and other inhumane weapons
- secure peace and democratic stability in Central America and the Caribbean
- develop military and police capabilities to protect both the natural environment and the use of financial resources.[17]

Political and economic policies must be congruent if the military and law enforcement systems of the hemisphere are to meet these objectives.

Hemispheric National Security Framework

Perfecting the hemispheric national security framework, and the US role in it, calls for a mix of political and military diplomacy. This topic is ranked first in priority because, while parts of the other nine agenda items are possible through bilateral and sub-regional accords and programs, the goal of a peaceful, democratic, and prospering Western Hemisphere requires a structure that no major sector of the world has even had: a multinational security roundtable without a perceived immediate foreign military threat. Circumstances are right for creating this mechanism.

Foster Military Professionalism

The immediate concomitant to the structural imperative is the strategy of fostering military and law enforcement professionalism. The conceptual dimension is a continuing process of cognitive (dealing with facts) and affective (dealing with values) professional education. The delivery means have existed in part for half a century. These are the US Army School of the Americas at Ft. Benning, Georgia; the Inter-American Air Force Academy at Lackland Air Force

Base, Texas; and the Naval Small Craft Instruction and Technical Training School at Rodman Navy Base in Panama. These three institutions all present, in Spanish, professional courses that use US curriculum models filtered through the platform delivery of a sophisticated inter-American faculty. Since the early 1960s the Inter-American Defense Board has operated the Inter-American Defense College (IADC), at Ft. McNair, in Washington, D.C. While not entirely analogous, the IADC in many ways resembles the NATO Defense College in Rome.[18]

Cognitive professional education is available to most Latin American military and police personnel through a wide spectrum of schools and foreign advisory mechanisms, both at home and abroad. What makes the IADC and the family of US-operated schools so valuable is the affective dimension of the education they provide. Students study military and police topics in Spanish, as the most universal of the region's native languages, sharing the experience with hemispheric classmates who face differing challenges but who share cultural bonds.[19] An officer or a sergeant can memorize a tactical or technical procedure in the cognitive domain, but one converts those procedures into functional morality and professionalism via the affective learning channel.

The existing family of US-operated professional military education schools should be expanded to permit all participating nations, not just the United States, to serve as teachers and role models. The Colombian army, for example, is a world leader in humane peacekeeping operations, both at home and abroad, with a long record of public affirmation to prove it. The Costa Rican civil guard and the Barbadian defense force are world-reputed models for the national defense institution in a small, democratic country. The Brazilian navy is effective in both fluvial and blue-water regional security operations. Canada and Colombia are world leaders in blue-helmet operations. In an expanded learning environment, these countries would share their areas of military and law enforcement success with officers and noncommissioned officers of the hemisphere.

US strategy should include the expansion and inter-Americanization of the School of the Americas concept to embrace several campuses in a variety of host countries. One campus, with a heavily civilian faculty, should offer a one-year professional foundations course, "Military and Police Professionalism in the Americas," with a strong curriculum in history, law, ethics, human rights, democracy, economics, and the inter-American system. A subculture of civilians from the Latin American defense and law enforcement ministries should attend these schools regularly with their military counterparts, just as US civilian security careerists now attend the Department of Defense family of senior service colleges. The hemispheric nations should be encouraged to provide modest financial support plus administrative machinery to encourage attendance at the courses and career tracking of the graduates.

Marginalize the Narco-traffickers

Reducing the violent and inherently destabilizing effects of the narcotics empires is a task that cuts across political, economic, and military interests. US strategy should acknowledge that much of the problem begins in the United States, among the cocaine users who have the cash to buy the drug.[20] Any counternarcotics strategy must recognize that Mexico or the Andean Region is just one facet of the worldwide supply and distribution network, and that any solution must attack the challenge at every level from grower to consumer.

The narcotics kingpins operate bogus nation-states, heavily armed and ruthless beyond description. Colombia alone, for example, has lost more troops in fighting the narco-traffickers since 1983 than the United States lost in all foreign conflict during the same period. Each of the three Inter-American networks for dialogue—political, economic, and military—must work for a coordinated solution that matches resources to measured effectiveness. The roundtable principle means that within Latin America, at least, US views on how to conduct anti-drug operations within sovereign countries would rest upon the wishes of the host nation.[21]

The drug scourge can never be ended; it is a dimension of human vice that can be changed only in degree through applied public policy. But much of the military training and force configuration that has proved useful in fighting the drug war is also appropriate for other military and security scenarios such as border control, disaster relief, anti-terrorism efforts, regional and international peace operations, and small coalition force campaigns.

Humane Migration Control

Coping with migration as a national security problem translates into close dialogue between armed forces and police forces. Armed forces participation on this topic may include the occasional dedication of surveillance, communications, and transportation equipment to back up what is clearly a law enforcement challenge. Several Latin American countries have paramilitary forces, such as the Venezuelan national guard and the Argentine national gendarmerie, who do these tasks skillfully; the US role in the regional effort would be to serve as supporting logistics provider, not as primary operator. US law enforcement agencies, such as the Customs and Immigration Service, the Drug Enforcement Administration, the Federal Bureau of Investigation, and state and local police organizations across the sunbelt states, should be major participants in this effort. Clearly, long-term victory over this particular challenge would be enhanced by the success of the GATT family of trade accords, especially NAFTA, CARICOM, and the Central American Common

Market. History suggests that there will always be problematic countries within a region, and therefore mass migration remains a mixture of humanitarian, legal, and national security challenges. The national security role in mass migration is professionally underdeveloped and should become a curriculum initiative within the hemispheric system of schools for military and police leaders.[22]

Sea Lanes, Air Lanes

The future strategic task on the seas adjacent to Latin America is to enhance the region's navies as they assume increased roles during an era of economic development and industrialization, without stimulating a costly and disruptive naval arms race. The blue-water navies of Argentina, Brazil, and Chile have been influential in the region since the 1880s. US naval captains have played a quiet role in bilateral and multilateral maritime diplomacy with these three navies ever since that era.[23] Just prior to World War II, US Navy policy added the Andean Region navies in coastal and blue-water security missions, and, as Cuba became a mid-range military threat late in the Cold War, the Caribbean navies joined US naval security activities in that sub-region.[24]

Latin America's air forces find their principal employment, at present, in logistical support of land forces. One of Latin America's most important decisions during the Cold War was not to emulate the airpower arms races in progress in the Middle East, much of Asia, parts of Africa, and all of Europe. The Andean Region air forces have roles in the anti-narcotics conflict, although the growth of national police forces in the region has brought about a proliferation of aviation assets among the national security forces, some of it duplicative and inefficient. While the role of the Latin American armed forces in developing a technical sector within the educational sphere is well known, a less known aspect is the role of the air forces in stimulating a multi-sectoral aviation industry.[25]

Discussion of future seapower and airpower strategies within Latin America during a time of economic growth must address the issue of persuading the region to take on a sense of importance about protecting the neutrality of the Panama Canal. Uncle Sam's motives about defending the neutrality of the Panama Canal always have evoked mixed perceptions in both the United States and in Latin America.[26] The Carter-Torrijos Treaties and the Cold War's end now offer the perfect opportunity for Washington to divest itself of this chronic national security dilemma. A future strategy is for US diplomats, in coordination with US air and sea officers, to encourage the region's own air forces and navies to proclaim and maintain the neutrality of the Panama Canal. The locus of Panamanian foreign relations concerns then becomes the OAS.

Military Civic Action and Blue-Helmet Operations

Enhancing Latin America's blue-helmet and civic action roles is a strategy of value to the region and to the world. The effectiveness of Colombian soldiers in Korea (1952-1954, UN) and in the Sinai (1956-1958, UN; 1981-present, Multinational Force and Observers) has caused village mayors in turbulent regions to ask for them by name.[27] Several measures would take advantage of the skills and experiences developed in those kinds of operations. First, curriculum units in peacemaking and peacekeeping operations, taught by Colombians and Canadians with actual blue-helmet experience, should be added to the curriculum of the hemispheric professional military schools. Second, as other nations join in the teaching process, a pilot staff for an Inter-American Defense Force (IADF) should be set up within the OAS Security Council. Third, the hemisphere's political and economic structures should be provided with a statement of capabilities and control measures for this IADF in order to defuse concerns about the force becoming a new kind of gunboat diplomacy.[28]

The civic action role for the Latin American military forces was well established, legally and morally, in the early 1960s.[29] Core curriculum programs at the hemisphere's professional military schools can highlight specific abuses that have occasionally tainted an otherwise excellent civic action record. Civic action programs should not compete with civilian economic activity, should only function where civilian government and the private sector cannot operate, and should not be used as a philosophical cover for military-operated arms factories. The maturation of democratic governmental institutions and free enterprise economic systems now alleviates many of these concerns in the region. The Colombian National Civic Action Council, where the Minister of Defense is the only voting military representative among 16 members, is the best functional model.[30] Civic action by military forces, done efficiently under civilian control, can be a vital contributor to Latin American regional economic and political development.

Guaranteeing Human Rights

The securing of human rights by the armed forces of the Americas is a universally attainable goal by the end of the 20th century. Human rights as an academic subject is taught at the School of the Americas. It is really a mixture of several international accords (Hague, 1907; Geneva, 1949), military and civil law of each country, and an expanding body of ideas based upon the United Nations Declaration of Human Rights. Public knowledge about the subject comes from government sources of mixed accuracy, international humanitarian groups such as the Red Cross, nongovernmental organizations (called "NGOs" in the literature) dedicated to human rights advocacy, news media sources of widely varying credibility, political groups often having ideological agendas, and criminal organizations such as the Andean narcotraffickers. While controversy and emotion attend every facet of the process, Latin America has produced legitimate, battle-decorated human rights heroes like General Manuel Sanmiguel Buenaventura of Colombia and police General Antonio Ketin Vidal of Peru; unfortunately, the deeds of these men rarely appear in the news.[31]

Developing respect for human rights among uniformed personnel lies more in the affective psychological domain than in the cognitive domain. Further, the contextual authority setting, the state of troop training, and the level of the armed threat all play strong roles. It is one thing to posture for the concept of human rights from the safety of the podium and quite another to place one's life at risk among murderous drug cartel gunmen. Each country needs training initiatives such as the 1993 contract between the Ecuadorian armed forces and the Latin American Association for Human Rights.[32] The hemisphere's armed forces could then share techniques for training troops in this matter, while their political counterparts ensure parallel commitment to human rights training by law enforcement agencies. The case for terminating US training assistance, currently called Enhanced International Military Education and Training (IMET), to punish Latin American human rights violators in uniform may be viewed as another example of the a priori assumption that all US military actions in the region are morally tainted, or are corrupted by exposure to the Latin American military profession.[33]

Arms Limitations

Latin America is the world's only region having no inventory of nuclear, biological, and chemical weapons. Despite some controversy in the 1980s about nuclear arms and nuclear power development in the Southern Cone, Latin America's governments without exception stand opposed to the existence of weapons of mass destruction in the region. Further, there is a strong initiative under way in Central America to remove the land mines implanted by several antagonists during the 1980s.[34] The US Army School of the Americas has trained packets of Latin American military and police to do some of this dangerous work. One of the strongest ways to build confidence in the region's armed forces and police is for all commanders to declare and show opposition to human rights violations and inhumane weapons.

Burying Hatchets

Putting to rest the earlier conflicts and repressions in Central America and the Caribbean is an agenda which cannot be avoided, if the proposed OAS Security Council is to be taken seriously. Burying old hatchets in Central America is not enough; new political and economic thinking, protected by a new breed of military and police personnel, is an urgent necessity. Those who work directly with Central America's younger generation of military officers see hopeful signs: armies are getting smaller, police forces are being created, and the rising junior officers in many forces now concern themselves with professionalism, not ideology. The hemispheric political community must give change a chance to occur. Demilitarization of former combatants in Nicaragua and El Salvador has been helpful and must continue; supervised electoral processes that seem to work must be affirmed by accompanying economic growth.[35]

Two current problems threaten the impulse to move away from armed interventions—the situation in Haiti and the continuing deterioration of Cuba under Castro. The United States must restrain the understandable urge to employ its own military force unilaterally in Haiti. A combination of coercive diplomacy and negotiation must first restore a constitutional government, and peacekeeping commitments must come from the hemisphere at large.[36] Training of a new Haitian police force by the Royal Canadian Mounted Police in 1993 and 1994 is precisely the right kind of foundation step required for ultimate success.

With regard to Cuba, military invasion would be the one certain way to foster Cuban and hemispheric sympathy for Fidel Castro and thereby lengthen his faltering stay in power. Any national security measures attending the ultimate collapse of Castro's regime must be hemispheric.[37]

In all these cases, the divisive leftist vs. rightist rhetoric pertaining to US policy in Latin America must be put aside if Uncle Sam is to retain post-Cold War leadership among equals in the region. Full but self-restrained participation in the triad of hemispheric political, economic, and military roundtables, however, constituted, is in the US national interest. US leaders and Latin American interest lobbies within the United States can scarcely expect Latin Americans to end feuds if US policy toward the region is made with moralistic zealotry.[38]

Environment and Resources

The Western Hemisphere's military leaders must become champions of the natural environment and of scarce economic resources within their countries. The dismal environmental record of the communist armed forces in Eastern

Europe and the former Soviet Union has sent the world a shocking message, one which probably helps nail down the coffin of Marxist ideology. Their unexploded shells, unregistered land mines, spilled toxic wastes, rusting junkyards, and crudely managed nuclear programs will cost the world countless casualties and billions of dollars in restoration. Similarly, the Western world's armed forces consume too much fuel, emit excess toxic wastes, and often fail to budget funds for cleaning up discarded military sites. Latin American militaries are not alone in having lessons to learn.

The Latin American armed forces already have done some good work in the environmental area. Brazilian troops have turned up in the frontier zones in recent years to confront environmental abusers who were laying waste the land and killing workers who dared to object. Colombian troops in the field have always been a model case for leaving their area of operations just a bit better than before they arrived.[39] Ecuadorian army troops were fighting fires in the Galapagos Islands in April 1994, rescuing one of the earth's most important natural habitats.

Resources management is another topic now taking root among the Western Hemisphere's armed forces and police. It is defined as the distribution of scarce resources among abundant alternatives; scholastically, it embraces microeconomics, decision science, operations research, scientific management theory, and cyclical budgetary processes. Like human rights, resources management must penetrate the affective realm of the learner to have value. The military officer or police commander must learn to do the most with the least, and to do rational cost and benefit analysis as a matter of routine. For Latin America's small armed forces, this could mean comparing five different ways to interdict border smuggling, combining the measures with illegal immigration control and the anti-narcotics campaign, and then blending the resources of land, sea, air, and police forces in the most effective, and hopefully efficient, mix. By stretching scarce cash during an era of economic privatization, the Latin American militaries can set a good example and help their governments provide desperately needed social services with the money not spent on military things.[40]

US Influence on the Region's Militaries

US land, sea, and air officers have done excellent work with Latin America. They have been perceived as helpful modernizers more than as invaders. Illustrious officers like Colonel George W. Goethals, General Leonard Wood, and General Matthew B. Ridgway served with distinction in Latin America long before the Cold War. General Ridgway figured prominently in the early days of the Inter-American Defense Board and the transition to Cold War policy era. General Vernon L. Walters was influential in linking Latin America's armed forces to appropriate Cold War roles. General John R. Galvin and General Frederick F. Woerner were senior Latin American experts during the height of the Cold War challenges; both officers served prominently in other theaters. General George A. Joulwan and General Barry R. McCaffrey combined military success in other world theaters with great knowledge of Latin America's changing security challenges at Cold War's end.

The US Navy and the US Marine Corps bore the brunt of US military policy in Latin America during the age of gunboat diplomacy (1870-1933). Both developed a cadre of senior officers who knew Latin America well, and who are remembered positively in the region despite the military interventionist roles they often played. The US Army was the major actor that linked Latin America to the Cold War challenges (1947-1989), mostly through countering armed subversion, and simultaneously served as role model and teacher for professionalization and acceptance of civilian authority. Those two missions were done with devotion and skill, and with limited resources, since neither had high priority for defense expenditures.

In the 1990s, the repository of US Army national security knowledge about Latin America must not be discarded for lack of a strategic initiative, nor lost through attrition of personnel. Working cooperatively with the other armed forces and federal law enforcement agencies, the US Army is the logical senior executive agent to carry out the ten strategic initiatives, to build the military linkage (*hermandad*) that will make the Americas, once and for all, the bastion of freedom and opportunity that George Washington and Simon Bolivar both fought to achieve and labored to build.

NOTES

[1] Henry M. Brackenridge, *Voyage to South America* (London: T. and J. Allman, 1820), pp. 212-16.

[2] Bernardo Jurado Toro, *Bolivar y la ley* (Caracas: Direccion de Artes Graficas M.D., 1991), pp. 166-68.

[3] David Bushnell, *The Making of Modern Colombia* (Berkeley: Univ. of California Press, 1993), pp. 55-56.

[4] Russell W. Ramsey, "The Spanish Military Orders: Alcantara, Calatrava, and Santiago," *Army Quarterly & Defence Journal*, 113 (June 1983), 345-46.

[5] Russell W. Ramsey, "A Military Turn of Mind: Educating Latin American Officers," *Military Review*, 73 (August 1993), 13.

[6] Literally, "power of the country"; contextual praxis connotes that the army may be used only for national defense, and police who answer to judges must be used for domestic law enforcement.

[7] John T. Currier, "The Role of Latin American Armed Forces in Peacekeeping Operations," unpublished paper, Troy State Univ. at Ft. Benning, March 1994, p. 3; and International Institute of Strategic Studies, *The Military Balance, 1993-1994* (London: IISS, 1994), pp. 253-60. Three of these peacekeeping forces are multinational but not under the United Nations.

[8] Russell W. Ramsey, "U.S. Military Courses for Latin Americans Are a Low-Budget Strategic Success," *North-South, the Magazine of the Americas*, 2 (February-March 1993), 38-41.

[9] Richard L. Sutter, "The Strategic Implication of Military Civic Action," in *Winning the Peace: The Strategic Implications of Military Civic Action*, ed. John W. DePauw and George A. Luz (New York: Praeger, 1992), pp. 185-89; and Russell W. Ramsey, "The Role of Latin American Armed Forces in the 1990s," *Strategic Review*, 20 (Fall 1992), reprinted in *Proceedings, 5th Latin American Conference* (Ft. Benning, Ga.: US Army School of the Americas, 1993).

[10] Timothy P. Wickham-Crowley, *Guerrillas & Revolutions in Latin America* (Princeton, J.J.: Princeton Univ. Press, 1992), pp. 68-85; and Jennifer Morrison Taw, "The Effectiveness of Training International Military Students in Internal Defense and Development," National Defense Research Institute (Santa Monica, Calif: RAND, 1993, pp. 15-22.

[11] US Congress, *Congressional Record*, Security Assistance Programs, Fiscal Year 1994 (Washington: GPO, 1994), pp. 3-16, 19-21, 38, 44-46, 48-60.

[12] Abraham F. Lowenthal, "Changing U.S. Interests and Policies in a New World," in *The United States and Latin American Relations in the 1990s: Beyond the Inter-American System*, ed. Jonathan Hartlyn, et al. (Chapel Hill:

Univ. of North Carolina Press, 1993), pp. 65-85. This article is easily the best short calculus of US strategic interests in Latin America.

[13] James R. Harding, "Security Challenges and Opportunities in the Americas," *North-South, the Magazine of the Americas*, 3 (February-March, 1994), 48-51.

[14] Peter Hakim, "NAFTA ... and After: A New Era for the US and Latin America?" *Current History*, 93 (March 1994), 97-102.

[15] Robert Devlin, *Debt and Crisis in Latin America: The Supply Side of the Story* (Princeton, J.J.: Princeton Univ. Press, 1992), 7-8, 253-56; and Sidney Weintraub, "The Economy on the Eve of Free Trade," *Current History*, 92 (February 1993), 72.

[16] J. Benjamin Zapatz, "The Honduran View," In Russell W. Ramsey, ed., *Proceedings, Eighth Latin America Symposium* (Maxwell AFB, Ala.: Air Command & Staff College, 1991), pp. 19-21. Minister-Counselor Zapatz's ability to explain national security in terms of the political economy is but one example of these economic "superstars" in action.

[17] Gabriel Marsella and Fred Woerner, "Mutual Imperatives for Change in Hemispheric Strategic Policy: Issues for the 1990s," in *Evolving US Strategy for Latin America and the Caribbean*, ed. L. Erik Kjonnerwood (Washington: National Defense Univ. Press, 1992), 56. The inventory of Inter-American strategic agenda items in this article is the most complete and coherent in the literature to date.

[18] "The Inter-American Defense College," *Military Review*, 50 (April 1970), 20-27.

[19] This explains the "Manuel Noriega Syndrome," namely, that the School of the Americans produced an academically superior graduate whose personal standards were vicious. Noriega avoided the affective education environment, filtering out useful technical information for his own purposes. All schools have conspicuous failures among their alumni.

[20] Russell W. Ramsey, "U.S. Narcotics Addiction Wrecks Colombian Democracy," *Army Quarterly & Defence Journal*, 120 (January 1990), 27-34. US cocaine cash intercepted in Colombia during 1990 was $1.2 billion dollars, the annual worldwide profit of Coca-Cola International that year.

[21] Kate Doyle, "The Militarization of the Drug War in Mexico," *Current History*, 92 (February 1993), 83-88; James Van Wert, "Bush's Other War," in *War on Drugs: Studies in the Failure of U.S. Narcotics Policy*, ed. Alfred W. McCoy and Alan A. Block (Boulder, Colo." Westview Press, 1992), pp. 27-34; Bruce M. Bagley and Juan G. Tokatlian, "Dope and Dogma: Explaining the Failure of U.S. Latin American Drug Policies," in *The United States and Latin American Relations in the 1990s: Beyond the Inter-American System*, ed. Jonathan Hartlyn, et al. (Chapel Hill: Univ. of North Carolina Press,

1992), pp. 214-33; and Kevin Dougherty, "The Role of the U.S. Military in Interdicting the Latin American Drug Traffic: How the Latin Americans See It," unpublished paper, Troy State Univ. at Ft. Benning, March 1994.

[22] Diego Ascencio, "Immigration and Economic Development for the 21st Century," in Kjonnerwood, pp. 147-58.

[23] Naval Ministry, *Gazetta de Noticias* (Rio de Janeiro), 12 October 1923, trans. US Dept. of State Serials File on Brazil, 1910-29, State Dept. archive code no. 823.20/34; and Armin K. Ludwig, "The Decades of Brazilian Geopolitical Initiatives and Military Growth," *Air University Review*, 37 (July-August 1986), 56-64.

[24] In 1915, Captain Edward L. Beach, US Navy, was commended by the Navy Department for averting great bloodshed in Haiti. He negotiated a truce between the armed forces of the principal rivals during a violent overthrow of the government, at great risk to his own life. See also Lars Schoultz, *National Security and United States Policy towards Latin America* (Princeton, J.J.: Princeton Univ. Press, 1987), pp. 199-215.

[25] Paul G. Havel, "The Role of Latin American Air Forces in Modernizing Society," unpublished paper, Troy State Univ. at Ft. Benning, March 1994; and Jorge A. del Carpio Tejeda, "La Policia Nacional en la Guerra Anti-narcotraficante en Peru" US Army School of the Americas, July 1993.

[26] Michael L. Connif, *Panama and the United States: The Forced Alliance* (Athens: Univ. of Georgia Press, 1992), pp. 169-71. A positive dimension of US policy in Panama is the training of the new Panamanian National Police by the International Criminal Investigative and Training Assistance Program, a US Department of Justice operation. The program is strictly concentrated upon law enforcement, not national defense. This policy represents an alternative national security training paradigm of great potential for other countries.

[27] Russell W. Ramsey, "The Colombian Battalion in Korea and Suez," *Journal of Inter-American Studies*, 9 (October 1967), 541-60.

[28] Robert A. Pastor, *Whirlpool: U.S. Foreign Policy toward Latin America and the Caribbean* (Princeton, N.J.: Princeton Univ. Press, 1992), pp. 287-89.

[29] H. H. Fischer, "Contribution de las Fuerzas Armadas en el Desarrollo Ecnomico-Social de los Paises," Inter-American Defense Board, Washington, D.C., 1 June 1961.

[30] Russell W. Ramsey, "Defensa Interna en los Anos 80: El Modelo Colombiano," *Military Review*, Spanish edition, 67 (July 1987), 62-77.

[31] Jaime Gonzalez Parra, "Gracias, Capitan," *El Tiempo*, Bogota, 27 April 1970, p. 2; and *Caretas* (Lima), 9 September 1992, p. 87.

[32] Ecuadorian Correspondent, "The Army Learns of Human Rights," *The Economist* (London), 16 October 1993, p. 49; and Jennifer M. Taw, "The

Effectiveness of Training International Military Students in Internal Defense and Development," National Defense Research Institute (Santa Monica, Calif.: RAND, 1993), pp. 15-22.

[33] Chalres Coll and Rachel Neild, "Issues in Human Rights," Paper #3 (Washington: Washington Office on Latin America, 1992), pp. 28-34. This analysis by a leading NGO sums up the pros and cons of training foreign military forces on moral topics.

[34] Kenneth Anderson and Stephen D. Goose, *Landmines, A Deadly Legacy* (New York: The Arms Project of Human Rights Watch, and Physicians for Human Rights, 1993), pp. 216-20.

[35] Richard L. Millett, "Central America's Enduring Conflicts," *Current History*, 93 (March 1994), 124-28.

[36] Pamela Constable, "Haiti: A Nation in Despair, a Policy Adrift," *Current History*, 93 (March 1994), 108-11. For the idea that Latin America's predisposition to place sovereignty above all other diplomatic values may be declining, see Richard J. Bloomfield, "Suppressing the Interventionist Impulse," in Richard J. Bloomfield and Gregory F. Treverton, *Alternative to Intervention: A New U.S.-Latin American Security Relationship* (Boulder, Colo.: Lynn Reinner, 1990), pp. 132-33.

[37] The most rational and compatible strategy to date appears in Gillian Gunn, *Cuba in Transition: Options for U.S. Policy* (Washington: Brookings Institution, 1993).

[38] Robert E. Toplin, "Many Latin Americanists Continue to Wear Ideological Blinders," *Chronicle of Higher Education*, 30 March 1994, p. A48.

[39] For indications that the Colombian public has long held their army in highest esteem, see Centro de Investigacion y Assion Social (CIAS), *Estructuras politicas de Colombia*, Coleccion "Monografias y Documentos," #3 (Bogota: CIAS, 1969), p. 5; and "Encuesta Nacional," *Semana* (Bogota), 11 January 1994, p. 55.

[40] The School of the Americas instituted a Resources Management Course in 1993, with the curriculum given at the Defense Resources Management Institute in Monterey, California, but tailored for Latin American application.

Russell W. Ramsey, Ph.D., D.Min.

On Castro and Cuba:
Rethinking the "Three Gs"
<u>Parameters</u> Winter 1994/5
RUSSELL W. RAMSEY

Emperor Charles I of Spain sent his bold *conquistadors* (conquerors) to the Americas in the early 16th century. Hernan Cortez subdued the Aztecs of Mexico, Francisco Pizarro wreaked havoc on the Incas of Peru, Gonzalo Jimenez de Quesada outfought the Chibchas of Colombia, and Pedro de Valdivia hounded the Araucanians of Chile, all in pursuit of the "three Gs": gold, glory, and God.

Four centuries later, the newly imperial-minded United States sent its troops to Cuba, which the previous generation of North Americans had just helped liberate from the threadbare remnants of Spain's dying empire. These new-breed *conquistadors* were men of a different genre: novelist and adventurer Ernest Hemingway, Olympic super-swimmer and Tarzan film star Johnny Weissmuller, over-the-hill Hollywood swashbuckler Errol Flynn, and the mobster casino chieftain Meyer Lansky. These men turned Cuba into North America's offshore playground and brothel, in the years before the sexual revolution in the United States made expensively scummy entertainment domestically accessible. Driven by new motivations in a different age, they redefined the "three Gs": gambling, girls, and glitz.

Monarchs Charles I and Philip II of Spain went on, after their conquest of Indo-America, to transform the region culturally into a giant Catholic empire with an army of priests and friars. Their Iberian-Catholic handiwork lasted politically for three centuries of relatively peaceful empire, held together by remarkably few soldiers. Creole-led revolutions for independence between 1810 and 1830 produced modern Latin America, the world's largest and oldest block of independent, constitutional nations, leaving Spain in control of Puerto Rico and Cuba. US forces liberated Cuba in 1898, during a thunderous moment of naïve idealism about exporting democracy. Cuba's reoccupation by the US neo-*conquistadores*, those proponents of the 20th century's "three Gs," created the conditions that allowed the illegitimate son of a wealthy Spanish immigrant to Cuba—one Fidel Castro—to become the primary thorn under the US national security blanket for 30 years. Never in his life a *campesino* (peasant), he became a global symbol of liberation, a romanticized champion of the poor. He overthrew a corrupt, inefficient army and replaced it with a revolutionary machine that challenged world powers on four continents. He outwitted US Presidents and Soviet Premiers with infuriating durability.

Ten important new works in the national security studies field examine the Cuban-US milieu during the Castro era. They are central to scholarship on the evolution of the US national security policy and strategy process between 1956 and 1991. But there is more at stake here than merely refighting the Cold War in the Caribbean. Fidel Castro virtually wrote the book on how a small power could play the superpowers against each other. While the world may not again organize itself into two militarily bristling supercamps, these books are excellent entries in a field often clouded by ideologically driven, murky scholarship. They offer reflections directly useful in the post-Cold War 1990s for US policy on Haiti, Panama, El Salvador, and Nicaragua; and they hold applications less geographically proximate for possible US roles in Bosnia, Cambodia, Iraq, Israel, North Korea, Rwanda, and Somalia.

Dozens of books purport to describe or explain the victory of Fidel Castro and his M-26 forces over Fulgencio Batista's regime in the late 1950s. The masterpiece in this genre is now Professor Thomas G. Paterson's *Contesting Castro: The United States and the Triumph of the Cuban Revolution.* Sparkling style and objectivity combine with sophisticated interpretation to answer satisfactorily, for the first time, the apparently unanswerable question: How did Castro win? Paterson's answer: Castro correctly identified the unseen legacy of shame and anti-US feeling among Cubans about the moral cesspool that sprang forth from the 20th-century version of the "three Gs." Then, while the US national security establishment, the Batista dictatorship, and the urban resistance to Batista conducted business during the period 1957-1959 with the organizational efficiency of the stars in a Three Stooges film, Castro built a disciplined power machine papered over with romantic liberationists innocence.

Professor Paterson's meticulous description of armed and violent challenges within Cuba, and the confused, clumsy responses to those challenges by Batista's forces and the US national security system is simply the best ever written. And this book emerged in 1994 when the US national security apparatus, supposedly 30 years more mature and sophisticated, was struggling desperately for solutions to comparable challenges in Bosnia, Haiti, Israel, Rwanda, and Somalia. There is no more Soviet Empire to swallow up revolutions gone awry in unstable developing countries, but the Three Stooges efficiency scenario seems to have peeked out from behind the US national security curtain again.

Once victorious, Fidel Castro led his revolution into the Soviet Union's camp, pounding the last coffin nails into the Monroe Doctrine. Triumphant at the botched 1961 Bay of Pigs invasion attempt by US-sponsored Cuban exiles, he was less clearly triumphant the following year after the 1962 missile crisis. Two new books now lay bare those chilling days with President John F. Kennedy directed his national security machinery personally, with mixed effectiveness.

Dino A. Brugioni was the chief electronic intelligence officer for the National Security Agency who unmasked the smuggling of strategic nuclear missiles and warheads into Cuba aboard Soviet cargo ships. His *Eyeball to Eyeball: The Inside Story of the Cuban Missile Crisis* is easily the best volume yet written on the complex world of technological intelligence and its interplay with the national security community. He offers the best insider description to date of what really went on in the Kennedy White House while the United States and the Soviet Union teetered at the brink of a global nuclear holocaust for a week. The book has obvious meaning for those charged with monitoring nuclear warhead development in Iraq and North Korea, and for those who track the inventory of Russia's still massive nuclear rocket array. It has even stronger meaning for those who receive technical intelligence estimates and convert them into national security decisions.

Scoffers at the notion that a nuclear war machine can be exported by clandestine means should study Anatoli I. Gribkov and William Y. Smith, *Operation ANADYR: U.S. and Soviet Generals Recount the Cuban Missile Crisis.* Here, with sincerity and objectivity, the Soviet general (Gribkov) in charge of smuggling nearly a hundred strategic nuclear missiles into Cuba in the summer of 1962 reveals how it was done. A US Air Force general (Smith) responds with the military side of the national security decision process in 1962. And one ponders: If the Soviet Union almost succeeded in setting up a deliverable inventory of nuclear rockets in Cuba, 90 miles from US soil in a small country having a US base within it, what pariah regime in the 1990s is reading the same book with the purpose of avoiding the Soviets' mistakes that led to detection?

For a Soviet view of Fidel Castro's place in international relations, the new standard is Yuri Pavlov's *Soviet-Cuban Alliance: 1959-1991.* Ambassador Pavlov served the former USSR as senior diplomatic representative in Cuba, Costa Rica, and Chile; as a Latin American specialist in the Foreign Ministry, he played a key role during the Cuban missile crisis. He and his colleagues in the Soviet national security community sincerely believed that Fidel Castro was implementing a new and authentic form of socialism in Cuba and abroad. However, he also suggests that Castro became a "communist of convenience" in 1960 to bolster his regime against US invasion. In the epilogue, he shows his disillusionment with revolutionary socialism as evidence of violent repression and mass terror mounted in Cuba. Pavlov's final words of warning about the inherently antidemocratic nature of radical revolutionaries would not be out of place as required reading in US political science and history classrooms.

What of Fidel Castro, the man, and his place in world history? Jules Dubois (1959), Manuel Urrutia Lleo (1964), Herbert L. Matthews (1969), Ernest Halperin (1972), Carlos Franqui (1984), and Tad Szulc (1986) are some of the better-known biographers of Fidel Castro. In the apparent twilight of Castro's reign comes Robert E. Quirk's *Castro, A Biography*, a volume which eclipses all the others in objectivity, research, and scope; it is likely to stand as the definitive work until Fidel Castro no longer rules Cuba. With meticulous documentation, Professor Quirk captures the color of his subject while weaving a sophisticated fabric of the key events; and he avoids the crippling tendency of most Castro analysts to position his book somewhere on the liberal-conservative spectrum of US opinion. This volume, coupled with the Paterson study, opens avenues for conceptualizing and assessing Fidel Castro's enormous effect on US national security policy since late 1958.

And what is to be done as *fidelismo* (political credence in Fidel) wanes in Cuba? Georgetown University Professor Gillian Gunn has published the most specific answer in her 1993 work *Cuba in Transition: Options for U.S. Policy*. Easily the best analyst of Cuban military operations in Africa during the 1980s, she now offers a rational agenda of carrots and sticks by which to bring the Cuban people out of the revised "three Gs" syndrome so well explained by Professor Paterson, and into the range of possibilities in *Latin America in a New World* edited by Professor Abraham F. Lowenthal and Gregory F. Treverton. The Cuba policy entry in the latter is "Cuba in a New World" by Professor Jorge I. Dominguez. For a range of views on current Cuba topics, Professor Donald E. Schulz offers another book called *Cuba and the Future*. The papers in the Schulz volume are the outcome of a January 1992 symposium at the Strategic Studies Institute of the Army War College, and the essay called "The Cuban Armed Forces in Transition" by Phyllis Greene Walker is a gem in the national security studies field.

For an independent yet complementary evaluation of the Cuban revolution and its recent adaptations to a changing world, Susan E. Eckstein's *Back From the Future: Cuba Under Castro* has balance and detail not found in other books. Her splendid 1994 analysis finds a Cuba not presented in political studies, a society that has evolved in ways that may reduce the passing of Fidel Castro to something non-catastrophic. Good but less unique is the eighth edition of Irving Louis Horowitz's interdisciplinary collection of essays, *Cuban Communism*. Jose Alonso's essay on the scapegoat execution of General Arnaldo Ochoa is strong, as is "The Politics of Psychiatry in Cuba" by Charles Brown and Armando Lago.

The US Army carried the institutional burden of working face-to-face with the Latin American military forces throughout the Cold War. Always there was the delicate balance to strike between fostering yet another repressive military regime and releasing a country to the Soviet Union's orbit. US Army leaders learned quickly from the mistakes committed in Fulgencio Batista's Cuba and moved on to a policy of selective equipping and quality training in the Spanish language. Despite the malignant and usually uninformed liberal-conservative dichotomy on US policy in Latin America, the region produced only one solid and enduring Marxist-Leninist regime during the Cold War, and that was Cuba. The books reviewed here suggest strongly that Fidel Castro's personal leadership coupled with the anti-US emotions rising from the revised "three Gs" agenda have more to say about Cold War Cuba than did Karl Marx.

BIBLIOGRAPHY

Dino A. Brugioni, *Eyeball to Eyeball: The Inside Story of the Cuban Missile Crisis*, Robert F. McCort, ed. (New York: Random House, 1991).

Jorge I. Dominguez, "Cuba in a New World," in Abraham F. Lowenthal and Gregory F. Treverton, *Latin America in a New World* (Boulder, Colo.: Westview Press, 1994).

Susan Eva Eckstein, *Back From the Future: Castro Under Cuba* (Princeton, J.J.: Princeton Univ. Press, 1994).

Anatoll I. Gribkov and William Y. Smith, *Operation ANADYR: U.S. and Soviet Generals Recount the Cuban Missile Crisis*, ed. Alfred Friendly, Jr. (Chicago: Edition q, 1994).

Gillian Gunn, *Cuba in Transition: Options for U.S. Policy* (Washington: Brookings Institute, 1993).

Irving Louis Horowitz, ed, *Cuban Communism* (8th ed.; New Brunswick, N.J.: Transaction Press, 1994).

Thomas G. Paterson, *Contesting Castro: The United States and the Triumph of the Cuban Revolution* (New York: Oxford Univ. Press, 1994).

Yuri Pavlov, *Soviet-Cuban Alliance: 1959-1991* (New Brunswick, J.J.: Transaction Press, 1994).

Robert E. Quirk, *Castro, A Biography* (New York: Norton, 1993).

Donald E. Schulz, ed., *Cuba and the Future* (Westport, Conn.: Greenwood Press, 1994).

The Reviewer: Lieutenant Colonel Russell W. Ramsey7 (USAR, Ret.), is Distinguished Resident Professor, US Army School of the Americas, Ft. Benning, Georgia. He is a graduate of the US Military Academy and holds a Ph.D. from the University of Florida. As a young Army captain in 1961, he wrote the curriculum for the first counterguerrilla course taught at the School of the Americas. In may 1961, as the new course was ready to begin, the young Captain Ramsey was surprised one night to hear Fidel Castro read his name during a four-hour radio harangue. Castro included Ramsey's name with a list of well-known organized crime figures, affirming that these men were "the new faculty who will train Latin American military men to murder the friends of the common people, another bloody plot of the US Army."

Russell W. Ramsey, Ph.D., D.Min.

Reading Up On the Drug War
Parameters Autumn 1995
RUSSELL W. RAMSEY

Readers can profit from a spate of books and articles about the world's struggle against narcotics. This literature can be grouped topically into investigative reporting, ideological cannon shots, and policy critiques. Some of the investigative reporting is so realistic that the reader feels drawn into the nether world of the narcotics culture. Some of the ideologically driven authors disguise their rapier thrusts with footnotes, quotations, and other scholarly apparatus, thereby giving the impression of an objective policy critique. And the more scientifically written policy studies pull the reader into columns of data and pithy little annotations about what CHI^2 really means in this case. One needs to be very focused to assess these books, for among them there is fascinating reading on a morbid, gripping, and sadly enduring topic.

Maria Jimena Duzan is a journalist with *El Espectador* (*The Spectator*) of Bogota, a splendid newspaper aligned generally with the Liberal Party. Her *Death Beat*, translated from the Spanish in 1994 by Peter Eisner, is simply the best book of our times on crime reporting. With hair follicles tingling, the reader wonders how an attractive, well-educated woman got close enough to the murderous subjects she investigated—Colombia's infamous cartel lords—with her objectivity and her life intact. In 1989, Guy Gugliotta and Jeff Leon of the *Miami Herald* staff produced the still relevant *Kings of Cocaine: Inside the Medellin Cartel*, focusing upon druglord Carlos Lehder. Again, the odor of exploding dynamite, the grins of the payoff goons, and the screams of the syndicate's torture victims all come alive, with lots of facts that stand up to later discovery. Max Mermelstein was the evil brain behind the Medellin cartel during that era. He spilled his guts about the infamous Ochoa brothers, Juan David and Fabio, to adventure another Robin Moore, who published the tale in 1990 as *The Man Who Made It Snow*. Arturo Carrillo Strong was a narcotics agent in the southwestern United States during the 1970s, when hard drugs of Latin American origin were becoming a plague. His memoir, *Corrido de Cocaina: Inside Stories of Hard Drugs, Big Money, and Short Lives*, appeared in 1990 and gives the reader a chilling longitudinal awareness of the street drug culture in the United States.

The value of reading these accounts lies in comprehending the milieu and the strength of the challenge before plunging into the policy critiques, where the clinical language somehow bypasses the wretched lives that are under discussion. And, let it be said, there are many other bestseller paperback gut spillers by drug culture participants of dubious veracity. The volumes mentioned above are marked by plausibility and good writing.

Jaime Malumud-Goti produced *Smoke and Mirrors: The Paradox of the Drug Wars* in 1992. While the US Drug Enforcement Administration indeed made mistakes during its pioneer Andean operations, both the DEA and the Bolivian armed forces and National Police learned from their mistakes. Malamud-Goti became so emotionally involved in defaming the supply side anti-drug policy of President George Bush that his account is unbalanced. Kevin Jack Riley, a scholar of demonstrated talent, also lost perspective while indicting the Colombian armed forces and police in his 1993 volume called *The Implications of Colombian Drug Industry and Death Squad Political Violence for U.S. Counternarcotics Policy.* He was partially duped by the syndicate propaganda machines: some of his villains are actually heroes of the anti-narcotics war.

Peter Dale Scott and Jonathan Marshall, an English professor and a newspaper staff financial analyst, wrote *Cocaine Politics: Drugs, Armies, and the CIA in Central America* in 1991. Already convinced that the 1980s conflicts in Nicaragua and El Salvador were contrived mercenary struggles initiated by President Ronald Reagan, these two apologists for the Nicaraguan Sandinistas and the El Salvadoran FMLN communist guerrillas indicted the drug war on similar lines. They discovered that there actually were no drug cartels in Latin America, nor even significant drug traffic save that being done by Reagan's "Contra" mercenaries in Nicaragua, General Manuel Noriega's Panamanian Defense Force, and the pro-US armies of Honduras and El Salvador. When this reviewer was a doctoral student in Latin American history, the University of California Press at Berkeley produced the leading scholarly works in the field. But their editorial decision to float this volume suggests a triumph of crudely ideological spin doctoring. Scott B. MacDonald's 1988 book, *Dancing on a Volcano*, for example, names most hemispheric druglords and is quite critical of US Andean drug policy; but it also shows clearly that Fidel Castro and his Sandinista allies in Nicaragua were selling drugs for cash to support their regimes in the 1980s.

There is plenty of room for scholarly writing that concludes US Andean drug enforcement policy to be a failure. The best short item on this theme is Bruce M. Bagley and Juan G. Tokatlian, "Dope and Dogma: Explaining the Failure of U.S.-Latin American Drug Policies," in Jonathan Hartlyn, Lars Schoultz, and Augusto Varas's 1992 edited volume, *The United States and Latin American in the 1990s: Beyond the Cold War.* The weak spot in Professor Bagley's thesis—that enforcement on the supply side is ineffective—is that no alternatiave is presented beyond a generic plea for a coordinated approach. Michael Kennedy, Peter Reuter, and Kevin Jack Riley show statistically in their 1994 study, *A Simple Economic Model of Cocaine Production*, that alternative cropping, often recommended as a better choice than crop eradication among traditional Andean cocaine growers, is economically unfeasible. Kevin Jack Riley's 1993 RAND Corporation study, *Snow Job? The Efficiency of Source Country Cocaine Politics*, shows convincingly that in-country interdiction alone cannot win.

Alfred W. McCoy and Alan A. Block draw upon worldwide examples from Asia, the Middle East, Africa, and Latin America in their 1992 volume of essays, *War on Drugs: Studies in the Failure of U.S. Policy*. But they offer no specific alternative, and their definition of failure is not always consistent. In 1993, veteran Pentagon policy analyst Carl H. Builder found in his book *Measuring the Leverage: Assessing Military Contributions to Drug Interdiction* that the problems of precise measurement and assessment were virtually insurmountable. Michael Childress would disagree, for he did a series of RAND Corporation studies which measure the drug trade with mistakes during its pioneer Andean operations, both the DEA and the Volivian armed forces and National Police learned from their mistakes. Malamud-Goti became so emotionally involved in defaming the supply side anti-drug policy of President George Bush that his account is unbalanced. Kevin Jack Riley, a scholar of demonstrated talent, also lost perspective while indicting the Colombian armed forces and police in his 1993 volume called *The Implications of Colombian Drug Industry and Death Squad Political Violence for U.S. Counternarcotics Policy*. He was partially duped by the syndicate propaganda machines: some of his villains are actually heroes of the anti-narcotics war.

Peter Dale Scott and Jonathan Marshall, an English professor and a newspaper staff financial analyst, wrote *Cocaine Politics: Drugs, Armies, and the CIA in Central America* in 1991. Already convinced that the 1980s conflicts in Nicaragua and El Salvador were contrived mercenary struggles initiated by President Ronald Reagan, these two apologists for the Nicaraguan Sandinistas and the El Salvadoran FMLN communist guerrillas indicted the drug war on similar lines. They discovered that there actually were no drug cartels in Latin America, nor even significant drug traffic save that being done by Reagan's "Contra" mercenaries in Nicaragua, General Manuel Noriega's Panamanian Defense Force, and the pro-US armies of Honduras and El Salvador. When this reviewer was a doctoral student in Latin American history, the University of California Press at Berkeley produced the leading scholarly works in the field. But their editorial decision to float this volume suggests a triumph of crudely ideological spin doctoring. Scott B. MacDonald's 1988 book, *Dancing on a Volcano*, for example, names most hemispheric druglords and is quite critical of US Andean drug policy; but it also shows clearly that Fidel Castro and his Sandinista allies in Nicaragua were selling drugs for cash to support their regimes in the 1980s.

There is plenty of room for scholarly writing that concludes US Andrean drug enforcement policy to be a failure. The best short item on this theme is Bruce M. Bagley and Juan G. Tokatlian, "Dope and Dogma: Explaining the

Failure of U.S.-Latin American Drug Policies," in Jonathan Hartlyn, Lars Schoultz, and Augusto Varas's 1992 edited volume, *The United States and Latin America in the 1990s: Beyond the Cold War*. The weak spot in Professor Bagley's thesis—that enforcement on the supply side is ineffective—is that no alternative is presented beyond a generic plea for a coordinated approach. Michael Kennedy, Peter Reuter, and Kevin Jack Riley show statistically in their 1994 study, *A Simple Economic Model of Cocaine Production*, that alternative cropping, often recommended as a better choice than crop eradication among traditional Andean cocaine growers, is economically unfeasible. Kevin Jack Riley's 1993 RAND Corporation study, *Snow Job? The Efficiency of Source Country Cocaine Politics*, shows convincingly that in-country interdiction alone cannot win.

Alfred W. McCoy and Alan A. Block draw upon worldwide examples from Asia, the Middle East, Africa, and Latin America in their 1992 volume of essays, *War on Drugs: Studies in the Failure of U.S. Policy*. But they offer no specific alternative, and their definition of failure is not always consistent. In 1993, veteran Pentagon policy analyst Carl H. Builder found in his book *Measuring the Leverage: Assessing Military Contributions to Drug Interdiction* that the problems of precise measurement and assessment were virtually insurmountable. Michael Childress would disagree, for he did a series of RAND Corporation studies which measure the drug trade with apparent precision. His 1994 work, *A System Description of the Cocaine Trade*, plus his 1993 studies with similar titles on heroin and marijuana should be read in conjunction with Builder's analysis. What emerges is the late Professor Hans Zetterbourg's oft-forgotten theory of the mid-range value in the social sciences. Global measurement yields statistical futility, and micro measurement produces precision about nothing that matters, so one picks the theory of the mid-range value. Childress's measurement parameters appear to be a healthy compromise between policy relevance and statistical precision.

Since a number of the studies concentrate heavily on the futility of fighting the drug war militarily in the Andes, through surrogate armies and police, one searches hopefully for some kind of study suggesting that the balanced approach—supply side interdiction at all levels, full court press against demand—may be working. The best exposition for the balanced attack is by Professor William O. Walker III, in a 1989 volume called *Drug Control in the Americas*. The Ohio Wesleyan University historian draws upon his research on little-known drug enforcement programs during the 1930s to make parallels with events in the 1980s. Professor Rensselaer W. Lee III argues in his 1991 book, *The White Labyrinth*, for the long-term, balanced approach. He examines bravely the case for legalization of addictive narcotics, concluding that such a policy would relieve some short-term problems at the expense of creating long-term social disasters.

Raphael F. Perl's 1994 study, *Drugs and Foreign Policy: A Critical Review*, may be the best single volume on how the illegal narcotics trade affects the US role in the world. It is complete, balanced, and much more objective than the earlier policy-bashing books, some of which are reviewed here. C. Peter Rydell and Susan S. Everingham carefully examined both supply side and demand side programs in their 1994 analysis, *Controlling Cocaine: Supply Versus Demand Programs*. A good analysis of US Andean drug strategy appeared in Peter H. Smith's 1992 collection of essays, *Drug Policy in the Americas*. Professor Smith shows clearly the policy conflicts that occur when the United States, a global military power whose own citizens are a major cause of the drug problem, attempts to fight a supply side war through a foreign army and police apparatus. But his essays also show signs of progress, and, more important, ways to form regional anti-narcotics partnerships.

Readers who find the drug policy literature depressing will want to check out the annual *National Drug Control Strategy* of the United States. Public Law 100-690 has required the production of this statement by the Office of National Drug Control Policy annually since 1989. Concise yet comprehensive, this document reduces the labyrinth of statistics, government agencies, legal jurisdictions, human rights in conflict, public health challenges, and the rest of the drug war maze to understandable detail. Drug strategies involve many issues which people simply do not want to face. Some of these are curtailment of civil liberties, acknowledging drug abuse in one's own family, hiring foreign armies and police to kill their own citizens, charges of moral hypocrisy by hemispheric neighbors, raising taxes to fund an unpopular program in a era of runaway national deficit, and dragging the armed forces into law enforcement just when the *posse comitatus* principle—armies for foreign defense only—is coming into acceptance worldwide.

In 1990, the word "coke" meant white addictive powder to some, and a crispy brown drink in a familiar bottle to others. In 1990, US citizens spent $1.2 billion for "coke" (cocaine) produced in Colombia; the Coca-Cola Corporation International earned #1.2 billion worldwide for its soft drink. The Colombian army and National Police have lost more personnel in the drug war since 1983 than the United States has lost in all combat operations since 1973. The challenges to national security in the post-Cold War era are, according to most experts, financial deficit and ethnic war in remote areas. Both of these challenges link strongly to the narcotics plague. Military professionals will find the 22 books, studies, and essays reviewed here of considerable value in understanding the reality that the armed forces are deeply involved in fighting the world's seemingly insatiable habit.

BIBLIOGRAPHY

Bagley, Bruce M., and Juan G. Tokatlian, "Dope and Dogma: Explaining the Failure of U.S.-Latin American Drug Policies," in Jonathan Hartlyn, Lars Schoultz, and Augusto Varas, eds., *The United States and Latin America in the 1990s: Beyond the Cold War*. Chapel Hill: Univ. of North Carolina Press, 1992.

Builder, Carl H. *Measuring the Leverage: Assessing Military Contributions to Drug Interdiction*. Santa Monica, Calif.: RAND, 1993.

Childress, Michael, Bonnie Dombey-Moore, and Susan Resetar. *A System Description of the Cocaine Trade*. Santa Monica, Calif.: RAND, 1994.

Childress, Michael. *A System Description of the Heroin Trade*. Santa Monica, Calif.: RAND, 1993.

Childress, Michael. *A System Description of the Marijuana Trade*. Santa Monica, Calif.: RAND, 1993.

Duzan, Maria Jimena. *Death Beat*, trans. Peter Eisner. New York: Harper Collins, 1994.

Gugliotta, Guy, and Jeff Leon. *Kings of Cocaine: Inside the Medellin Cartel*. New York: Simon & Schuster, 1989.

Kennedy, Michael, Peter Reuter, and Kevin Jack Riley. *A Simple Economic Model of Cocaine Production*. Washington: National Defense Research Institute, 1994.

Lee, Rensselaer W., III. *The White Labyrinth*. New Brunswick, N.J.: Transaction, 1991.

MacDonald, Scott B. *Dancing on a Volcano*. Westport, Conn.: Praeger, 1988.

Malamud-Goti, Jaime. *Smoke and Mirrors: The Paradox of the Drug Wars*. Boulder, Colo.: Westview Press, 1992.

McCoy, Alfred W., and Alan A. Block, eds. *War on Drugs: Studies in the Failure of U.S. Policy*. Boulder, Colo.: Westview Press, 1992.

Mermelstein, Max, as told to Robin Moore and Richard Smitten. *The Man Who Made It Snow*. New York: Simon & Schuster, 1990.

Perl, Raphael F. *Drugs and Foreign Policy: A Critical Review*. Boulder, Colo.: Westview Press, 1994.

Riley, Kevin Jack. *The Implications of Colombian Drug Industry and Death Squad Political Violence for U.S. Counternarcotics Policy*. Washington: National Defense Research Institute, 1993.

Riley, Kevin Jack. *Snow Job? The Efficiency of Source Country Cocaine Politics*. Santa Monica, Calif.: RAND, 1993.

Rydell, C. Peter, and Susan S. Everingham. *Controlling Cocaine: Supply Versus Demand Programs*. Santa Monica, Calif.: RAND, 1994.

Scott, Peter Dale, and Jonathan Marshall. *Cocaine Politics: Drugs, Armies, and the CIA in Central America*. Berkeley: Univ. of California Press, 1991.

Smith, Peter H., ed. *Drug Policy in the Americas.* Boulder, Colo.: Westview Press, 1992.

Strong, Arturo Carrillo. *Corrido de Cocaina: Inside Stories of Hard Drugs, Big Money, and Short Lives.* Tucson, Ariz.: Harbinger House, 1990.

US Office of National Drug Control Policy. *National Drug Control Strategy.* Washington: GPO, 1989-1994.

Walker, William O., III. *Drug Control in the Americas.* 2nd ed.; Albuquerque: Univ. of New Mexico Press, 1989.

The Reviewer: Russell W. Ramsey is a civilian professor at the US Army School of the Americas. He h olds the Ph.D. degree in Latin American history from the University of Florida and has written many articles on books on Latin American military topics.

Russell W. Ramsey, Ph.D., D.Min.

Strategic Reading on Latin America: 1995 Update
Parameters Winter 1995/6
RUSSELL W. RAMSEY

Appraising comparatively the post-Cold War national security literature on Latin America in my essay "Strategic Reading on Latin America" (*Parameters*, Summer 1994), made sense intellectually in view of the quest for a new paradigm. One year later, two clearly opposed viewpoints are established: the neo-liberal optimists and the neo-collectivist pessimists. Both voices merit the careful attention of strategists and national security architects.

Setting the Sails

Pierre Etienne Dostert's *Latin America 1994* is the best one-volume regional description in the English language. The earlier annual issues still read with authenticity since their origin in 1967. Part of the unique Stryker-Post "World Today" series on the world's regions, the Latin America volume integrates economic, political, and military trends and gives a menu for deeper reading. Longer and more topically oriented is *Security, Democracy, and Development in U.S.-Latin American Relations* (1994, edited by Lars Schoultz et al.). Where Dostert shows the restrained case for the neo-liberal optimist view, Schoultz and his author team are guarded pessimists, with an occasional glimpse of the neo-Marxist themes oft trumpeted by US Latin Americanists in the 1980s. William W. Finan, Jr., displays an intellectual reversal and a structural peregrination of importance to regional security issues. His February 1995 *Current History* issue on Latin America is a gloomy appraisal indeed, in contrast with his hopeful March 1993 Latin America issue. And he has thrown his hat into the ring on the contentious old debate over what defines Latin America; since the early 1500s scholars have disputed the geographic, political, ethic, linguistic, economic, religious, and cultural determinants of the region. Editor Finan has dedicated his March 1995 issue of *Current History* to an assessment of *North America including Mexico*, a paradigm guaranteed to sting both Ross Perot and the enthusiasts of regional *indigenismo* (translate as "native Americanism") and *Hispanidad* (translate as "Hispanic pride").

National security specialists were long hampered by the relatively fuzzy strategic literature on Latin America. Ironically, in the post-Cold War era there are now three research tools available to those who would calculate power questions about arms, soldiers, money, and resources. The volume *South*

America, Central America, and the Caribbean: 1995, from the 5th edition (1994) of Europa Publications' Regional Surveys of the World, is simply the most comprehensive thing of its kind ever done. This organization also puts out the world's oldest military journal, the (British) *Army Quarterly & Defence Journal*, famous since its founder, the Duke of Wellington, demanded the strategic integration of political, military, and economic affairs. Europa's British rival series, known colloquially as "Brassey's Annuals," offers *The Military Balance* from the International Institute of Strategic Studies, and the "Caribbean and Latin America" section in the 1994-1995 volume is the strongest current analysis on Latin America's greatly reduced and rapidly changing military institutions. Professor Claude C. Sturgill's three Latin American chapters in *The Military History of the Third World Since 1945* (1994) is the best work yet done on US security assistance linkage with the military institutions of all the world's developing regions.

Economics: The Science No Longer Dismal

A big movement in Latin American studies not applauded by many academics is the arrival of business administration experts and applied economists. Your reviewer, a historian, welcomes this development, having watched his history colleagues, the social scientists, and the humanists miss the interpretive boat on Latin America for four decades by stressing politics and ideology at the expense of economics. A lively economic literature now emerges, one that is definitely not a dismal science.

Paul W. Drake has edited *Money Doctors, Foreign Debts, and Economic Reforms in Latin America from the 1890s to the Present* (1994). Part of the impressive new Jaguar series from Scholarly Resources, Inc., the essays show how Latin America has been affected by classical laissez-faire commerce, positivism, Keynesian ideas, wartime commodity price guarantees, structuralism and statist economics, neo-Marxism and dependency theory, foreign investment and multinational corporations, raging inflation and indebtedness, mass unemployment, and now the neo-liberal philosophy of privatization and tariff minimization. If Drake's readings tip slightly toward the historical side, readers may spot a more purely economic viewpoint in William C. Smith et al., *Latin American Political Economy in the Age of Neoliberal Reform: Theoretical and Comparative Perspectives for the 1990s* (1994), again part of an excellent series, this one from the University of Miami North-South Center.

Jaime Suchlicki, editor of *North-South: The Magazine of the Americas*, devoted the entire November-December 1994 issue to the December 1994 Economic Summit of the Americas in Miami. Several of the articles relate trade and privatization to national security issues. Sadly, *North-South Magazine* ceases to exist with that issue, which will stand for years as a period statement on Latin American policy questions.

Soldiers & Cops in New Roles

Linda Alexander Rodriguez has edited *Rank and Privilege: The Military and Society in Latin America* (1994), another gem from the Jaguar series. These essays fill the vacuum on such questions as how the great *caudillos* (strongmen) gave way to professional military officers in the 20th century, and whence came the cultural ethos of the Latin American military officer. Professor Rodriguez introductory essay is definitive and should be incorporated into a general book of readings on the region. The annotated bibliography is the best short piece of its kind in print. G. Pope Atkins, Professor Emeritus at Annapolis, offers a new 1995 update of his *Latin America in the International Political System*, still the best regional entry in its field.

Scoffers at the notion that Latin America's men-at-arms have changed fundamentally will support Brian Loveman's "'Protected Democracies' and Military Guardianship: Political Transitions in Latin America, 1978-1993," in the *Journal of Interamerican Studies and World Affairs* (Summer 1994). In meticulous detail, he categorizes the countries of the region by the degree to which their armed forces accept civilian control over the military forces in several areas, and he concludes that most of them are still *golpistas* (soldiers who overthrow governments) at heart. Pericles Gasparini Alves examines Latin American regional arms limitation and military role restructuring in his edited volume *Proceedings of the Conference of Latin American and Caribbean Research Institutes, 2-3 December 1991, Sao Paulo* (1993). Discussions relating weapons and defense to economic development are excellent. Carlos Molina Johnson has often defended in modern words the doctrine of Diego Portales, a 19th-century Chilean cabinet minister, who argued that it is correct for the armed forces to guarantee a constitutional form of government by force, if necessary. In Molina's "Iberoamerica 2001," published in the School of the America's magazine *Adelante* (Summer 1992), he outlines the several roles for Latin America's armed forces in the next century. A similar taxonomy of future Latin American military roles is offered by Venezuela's Virgilio Rafael Beltran in "La Seguridad Hemisferica y el Nuevo Orden International," *Military Review* (Hispanic ed., September-October 1992). The political economist Margaret Daly Hayes reveals some positive and generally unknown trends in South American naval affairs in her 1995 study *By Example: The Impact of Recent Argentine Naval Activities on Southern Cone Naval Straategies*.

For a US academic appraisal of what soldiers and police south of the Rio Grande ought to be doing, see Gabriel Marcella's edited volume *Warriors in*

Peacetime: The Military & Democracy in Latin America (1994). He is less pessimistic than Loveman, to be sure, but also less rosy than Molina and Beltran. And he offers a short menu of his ideas on this vital topic in his essay "Forging New Strategic Relationships" which appeared in *Military Review* (October 1994). William Perry and Max Primorac pull in US regional security policy with their essay "The Inter-American Security Agenda" appearing in the *Journal of Interamerican Studies and World Affairs* (Fall 1994), as does our present reviewer in his article "US Strategy for Latin America" in *Parameters* (Autumn 1994).

And Still From the Left...

Scholars looking at leftist influence and security threats within Latin America during the Cold War tend to divide into two groups: those who applaud or bewail the demise of the radical left, and those who find it alive but differently arrayed.

Barry Carr and Steve Eliner edited *The Latin American Left: From the Fall to Allende to Perestroika* (1993), one of many titles from Westview Press on the interplay of leftist revolution and national security policy in Latin America. While they are not ready to abandon some of the heady romanticism which gave US academics an exaggerated view of Karl Marx's influence in Latin America during the Cold War, they nonetheless make a solid case for the part played by the political left in bringing about the era of political pluralization and economic privatization. For a more purely descriptive view, see Marcelo Cavarozzi, "The Left in Latin America: The Decline of Socialism and the Rise of Political Democracy," in Jonathan Hartlyn et al., *The United States and Latin America in the 1990s: Beyond the Cold War* (1992). Finally, for an unrepentant view that the far left has done mighty things with more still to come, read Eric Selbin's *Modern Latin American Revolutions* (1993), another Westview title.

Individual Security Topics

Donald E. Schulz and Deborah Sundloff Schulz coauthored in 1994 *The United States, Honduras, and the Crisis in Central America*, still another Westview volume. While focused upon war's havoc in Honduras during the 1980s, the authors achieve a coherent portrayal of the Central American region. It is meticulously supported and forms a caveat to future US Presidents who might decide to go a-filibustering once more. Louis W. Goodman and Gabriel Marcella have edited a short summary of their *Conference on Peace and Reconciliation in El Salvador, Sept. 8-9, 1994*, a joint product of the American University School of International Service Democracy Project and the US Army War College. A full-length volume containing the speeches is projected and would be a great contribution to scholarship.

Anthony P. Maingot shows why he is the emerging dean of Caribbean scholarship in the United States with his 1994 title *The United States and the Caribbean*, one of Westview's best ever. Maingot's article on Haiti in the February 1995 issue of *Current History* (previously mentioned herein) is a classic. Two other pieces on the recent US/UN operation in Haiti accompany the Maingot article. An excellent set of essays on Haiti by a mix of diplomats and scholars is found in Georges A. Fauriol, ed., *Haitian Frustrations: Dilemmas for U.S. Policy* (1995). This reviewer's "On Castro and Cuban Rethinking the 'Three Gs,'" appeared in *Parameters* (Winter 1994-1995). Ten blue-chip national security pieces on the future of Fidel Castro and his role in the Cold War are reviewed there in detail. The October-November 1993 issue of *North-South: The Magazine of the Americas* was devoted to trends in the southern cone: Argentina, Brazil, and Chile. Subsequent events have shown those articles to have been prescient indeed. Your present reviewer's "Reading Up On the Drug War" in *Parameters* (Autumn 1995) puts that melancholy literature into three categories: participant accounts, policy analysis, and political soapbox oratory.

Barry L. Brewer finds positive linkage between US military training conducted in Spanish for Latin American armed forces, and the long-range growth of professionalism. His study is called *U.S. Security Assistance Training of Latin American Militaries: Intentions and Results* (1995). Your reviewer's article "Forty Years of Human Rights Training" (*Journal of Low Intensity Conflict*, Autumn 1995) examines this sensitive topic in the context of Hemispheric involvement in the Cold War.

Books in Series

In the 1950s Columbia University's Professor Lewis Hanke edited a series of topical books in English on Latin America, known as the Borzoi series (Alfred A. Knopf Publisher). They were the first affordable paperbacks on the region, and the scholarship was superb. For military and national security professionals, several of the Borzoi classics are still germane. Huge M. Hamill, Jr., edited *Dictatorship in Latin America*; Luis E. Aguilar edited *Marxism in Latin America*; and British historians R. A Humphreys and John Lynch edited *The Origins of the Latin American Revolutions, 1808-1826*. Donald M. Dozer edited *The Monroe Doctrine: Its Modern Significance*, and Marvin Bernstein assembled *Foreign Investment in Latin America*. The series contained edited memoirs of foreign visitors to the region, and several volumes of collected essays on key countries such as Cuba, Mexico, and Brazil. Now, in the post-Cold War environment, come three excellent series of books on Latin America.

The Scholarly Resources Press of Wilmington, Delaware, offers its Jaguar Series under the editorship of William H. Beezley and Colin M. MacLachlan. Richard Hopper, Editorial Director at Scholarly Resources, is the architect of the series. The North-South Center at the University of Miami, under the leadership of Ambler H. Moss, Jr., has no single name for its recent books on security and economic issues in Latin America. But the titles recently edited by William C. Smith and reviewed herein constitute a topical series of great merit. The North-South Center's *Journal of Interamerican Studies and World Affairs* remains the best thing of its kind. Finally, the Westview titles continue to appear with regularity, and they seem to veer from their previous ideological trendiness into ramparts more enduring.

The Stryker-Post World Today series provides dependable and affordable country-by-country introductions, regionally organized. While the Latin America volume has been excellent since 1966, one gets a better perspective of Latin America by reading the other Stryker-Post works on Asia, Africa, the Middle East, and Europe. *Military Review*, of the US Army Command and General Staff College, continues to feature regular and excellent pieces on Latin America; its Spanish and Portuguese language editions carry different articles and play a vital hemispheric role in education and outreach.

Perhaps the most optimistic news is that the demise of the Cold War seems to have fostered a better quality of military and national security issues literature on Latin America than existed from 1947 to 1989. Since failure to understand those issues led to policy blunders by the United States during the Cold War, the trend bodes well for those who love peace, democracy, and economic plenty.

BIBLIOGRAPHY

Atkins, G. Pope. *Latin America in the International Political System.* 3d ed. Boulder, Colo.: Westview Press, 1995.

Alves, Pericles Gasparini, ed. *Proceedings of the Conference of Latin American and Caribbean Research Institutes 2-3 December 1991. Sao Paulo.* Geneva: United Nations Institute for Disarmament Research, 1993.

Beltran, Virgilio Rafael. "La Seguridad Hemisferica y el Nuevo Orden Internacional." *Military Review*, Hispanic ed. (September-October 1992), 2-17.

Brewer, Barry L. *U.S. Security Assistance Training of Latin American Militaries: Intentions and Results.* Wright-Patterson Air Force Base: US Air Force Institute of Technology, 1995.

Carr, Barry, and Steve Eliner, eds. *The Latin American Left: From the Fall of Allende to Perestrolka.* Boulder, Colo.: Westview Press, 1993.

Cavarozzi, Marcelo. "The Left in Latin America: The Decline of Socialism and the Rise of Political Democracy." In *The United States and Latin America in the 1990s: Beyond the Cold War*, ed. Jonathan Hartlyn et al. Chapel Hill: Univ. of North Carolina Press, 1992. 101-127.

Chipman, John, ed. "The Caribbean and Latin America." In *The Military Balance, 1994-1995.* London: International Institute of International Studies, 1994. 194-222.

Dostert, Pierre Etienne. *Latin America, 1994.* The World Today Series. Harper's Ferry, W. Va.: Stryker-Post Publications, 1994.

Drake, Paul W., ed. *Money Doctors, Foreign Debts, and Economic Reforms in Latin American from the 1890s to the Present.* The Jaguar Series. Wilmington, Del.: Scholarly Resources, 1994.

Fauriol, Georgia A., ed. *Haitian Frustrations: Dilemmas for U.S. Policy.* Washington: Center for Strategic and International Studies, 1995.

Finan, William W., Jr., ed. *Current History* (February 1995 "Latin America," and March 1995 "North America").

Goodman, Louis W., and Gabriel Marcella eds. *Proceedings of the Conference on Peace and Reconciliation in E. Salvador, Sept. 8-9, 1994.* Washington: American Univ. School of International Service Democracy Project, 1995.

Hayes, Margaret Daly. *By Example: The Impact of Recent Argentine Naval Activities on Southern Cone Naval Strategies.* Alexandria, Va.: Center for Naval Analyses, 1995.

Loveman, Brian. "'Protected Democracies' and Military Guardianship: Political Transitions in Latin America, 1978-1993." *Journal of Interamerican Studies and World Affairs* (Summer 1994), 105-89.

Maingot, Anthony P. *The United States and the Caribbean.* Boulder, Colo.: Westview Press, 1994.

Marcella, Gabriel. "Forging New Strategic Relationships." *Military Review* (October 1994), 31-42.

Marcella, Gabriel, ed. *Warriors in Peacetone: The Military & Democracy in Latin America.* Portland, Ore.: Frank Cass, 1994.

Molina Johnson, Carlos. "Iberoamerica 2001." *Adelante* (Summer 1992), 17-24.

Perry, William, and Max Primorac. "The Inter-American Ssecurity Agenda" *Journal of Interamerican Studies and World Affairs* (Fall 1994), 111-27.

Ramsey, Russell W. "Forty Years of Human Rights Training." *Journal of Low Intensity Conflict* (Autumn 1995).

Ramsey, Russell W. "On Castro and Cuba: Rethinking the 'Three Gs.'" *Parameters*, 24 (Winter 1994-1995), 138-41.

Ramsey, Russell W. "Reading Up On the Drug War." *Parameters*, 25 (Summer 1995), 104-07.

Ramsey, Russell W. "Strategic Reading on Latin America." *Parameters*, 24 (Summer 1994), 133-36.

Ramsey, Russell W. "US Strategy for Latin America." *Parameters*, 24 (Autumn 1994), 70-83.

Rodriguez, Linda Alexander, ed. *Rank and Privilege: The Military and Society in Latin America*. The Jaguar Series. Wilmington, Del.: Scholarly Resources, 1994.

Schoultz, Lars, William C. Smith, and Augusto Varas, eds. *Security, Democracy, and Development in U.S.-Latin American Relations*. University of Miami, North-South Center Series. New Brunswick, N.J.: Transaction Publishers, 1994.

Schulz, Donald E., and Deborah Sundloff Schulz. *The United States, Honduras, and the Crisis in Central America*. Boulder, Colo.: Westview Press, 1994.

Selbin, Eric. *Modern Latin American revolutions*. Boulder, Colo.: Westview Press, 1993.

Smith, Silliam D., Carlos Acuna, and Eduardo Gamarra, eds. *Latin American Political Economy in the Age of Neoliberal Reform: Theoretical and Comparative Perspectives for the 1990s*. University of Miami North-South Center Series. New Brunswick, N.J.: Transaction Publishers, 1994.

South America, Central America, and the Caribbean: 1995. Europa Publications' Regional Surveys of the World. 5th ed.; London: Europa Publications, 1994.

Sturgill, Claude C. "The Caribbean" (131-142), "Central America" 143-170), and "South America" (171-194). In *The Military History of the Third World Since 1945: A Reference Guide*. Westport, Conn.: Greenwood Press, 1994.

Suchlicki, Jaime, ed. *North-South: The Magazine of the Americas* (October-November 1993, "The ABCs;" and November-December 1994, "Summit of the Americas 1994 Miami"), publication of the North-South Center, University of Miami.

The Reviewer: Dr. Russell W. Ramsey is Distinguished Resident Professor at the US Army School of the Americas, Ft. Benning, Georgia.

Strategic Reading on Latin America:
Long on Quality, New Rumbles from the Left
<u>Parameters</u> Winter 1996/7
RUSSELL W. RAMSEY

In the post-Cold War era the need for rational consideration of ends-means linkage and the possible use of military force in the Latin American region is unclear. Ironically, the strategic literature on Latin America in 1996 is much better in quality than at any time during the Cold War, even though the Cold War produced a menu of issues that most national security analysts considered to be more truly "strategic."

An admittedly arbitrary menu of books and articles for 1996 can be organized into four categories: interpretive, US policy, anti-drug war, and Cuba and the radical left. This article is an update on previous offerings by your reviewer in *Parameters*: "Strategic Reading on Latin America" (Summer 1994), and "Strategic Reading on Latin America: 1995 Update" (Winter 1995-96).

Interpretive Works

The best starting point for analyzing Latin America's post-Cold War boom in privatization and democratic pluralization is the unheralded 1974 volume *Beyond Cuba: Latin America Takes Charge of Its Future*, edited and largely authored by Luigi Einaudi. Professor Einaudi et al. opined, under sponsorship of the RAND Corporation during a low point in US foreign relations, that Latin America would opt for constitutional democracy and a mixture of regulated free economies. They also held that the flamboyant militarism of the day was an evolving institution, its blatant interventionism caused by Latin America's entrapment in the Cold War, coupled with too-rapid urbanization amid weak civilian bureaucratic structures. Einaudi subsequently became US Ambassador to the Organization of American States (1989-1993) and is now a senior Latin America policy adviser. His 1974 book is to the post-Cold War interpretation of Latin America what Ambassador George Kennan's "Mr. 'X'" article in *Foreign Affairs* was to the Cold War: seminal, prophetic, and unique.

The best one-volume summary of the Latin American region is Pierre Etienne Dostert's *Latin America 1996*, the 30th edition in Stryker-Post's excellent World Today Series. Maps, bibliography, intellectual balance, photographs, good writing, and low price all combine to make this the textbook of choice for regional introductory courses. Abraham F. Lowenthal and Gregory F. Treverton are author-editors of *Latin America in a New World* (1994). These essays do the best job of relating politics, economics, and national security issues. Scott B. MacDonald et al. are the authors and editors of *Fast Forward: Latin America on the Edge of the Twenty-First Century*. Produced in 1996 at the Washington (D.C.) Center for Strategic and International Studies, these essays mix sound regional analysis with the Heidi and Alvin Toffler futuristic scenario; this volume and the Lowenthal work are good candidates for seminar textbooks at the war college and staff college levels, and for graduate programs in regional area studies. Your reviewer's piece "Latin American Military Affairs" in the March-April 1996 issue of *Military Review* evaluates several new strategic reference volumes of interest to the national security affairs student.

David Sheinin has written a 1995 work called *The Organization of American States*, a welcome addition that shows the regional organization's efforts in democracy-building, peace-making, and treaty negotiations. Another welcome and long overdue book is a 1995 collection of essays authored or edited by William H. Swatos entitled *Religion and Democracy in Latin America*. The role of evangelical Protestantism is fully evaluated, the changing nature of Roman Catholicism is examined, and liberation theology is put into a balanced context. The relationship between economic motivations and political behavior is analyzed closely in a 1992 study called *The Economics of Violence in Latin America: A Theory of Political Competition*, by Wilber A. Chaffee, Jr.

Howard J. Wiarda gives his customary balanced judgment to the politico-economic relationships in "After Miami: The Summit Crisis, the Peso Crisis, and the Future of U.S.-Latin American Relations," in the Spring 1995 issue of the *Journal of Interamerican Studies and World Affairs*. Benjamin Keen presents, in 1996, the sixth edition of his distinguished textbook, *Latin American Civilization: History and Society, 1942 to the Present*. It contains beautifully edited translations of the writings of key figures throughout Latin American history. Beginning Latin American history students in the United Sates, however, are going to get a highly unbalanced treatment if this becomes their only textbook, for Professor Keen has chosen to include only the writings of the democratic and revolutionary political left in his section on recent decades. Finally, your reviewer sorted out recent books on Latin America into two schools of thought in an essay called "Hopeful Neoliberals, Derailed Collectivists— Emerging Paradigms on Latin America," in the January-March 1996 issue of *Comparative Strategy*.

On US Policy

David W. Dent made a huge contribution to Western Hemispheric scholarship in 1995 by editing *U.S.-Latin American Policymaking: A Reference Handbook*. It is the first objective, systematic treatment of the US national security process as it affects Latin America, and it becomes the reference tool of choice for scholars in this field. A companion volume for the library of all institutions teaching US-Latin American relations is another 1995 offering, a collection of essays edited by John D. Martz under the title *United States Policy in Latin America*. Finally, Howard J. Wiarda's *Democracy and Its Discontents: Development, Interdependence, and U.S. Policy in Latin America* (1995) is arguably the best volume by a single author ever done on contemporary US policy in Latin America.

Four journal articles highlight strategic application of these three excellent books. Raymond M. O'Brien's "Regional Security in Latin America: U.S. Economic and Military Options," in the Fall 1992 issue of *Strategic Review*, is a Mahanist analysis. Paul G. Buchanan wrote "U.S. Defense Policy for the Western Hemisphere: New Wine in Old Bottles, Old Wine in New Bottles, or Something Completely Different?" in the *Journal of Inter-American Studies & World Affairs* (Spring 1996), and your reviewer offered "US Strategy for Latin America" in the Autumn 1994 issue of *Parameters*. These articles present US regional strategy essentially as applied military policy. Walter S. Clarke and Arthur E. Dewey crafted "Peace/Humanitarian Operations: Introducing the 'Comprehensive Campaign Plan,'" a 1996 paper based on their work in Latin America that is well worth reading.

Since the US Army took on a tutorial role with the Latin American armies during World War II, and gradually included the region's internal security forces in its doctrinal training umbrella, US policy toward the Latin American armed forces has been a critical issue for national security students. Geoffrey B. Demarest discusses the *passe comitatus* principle, under which armed forces defend the national sovereignty and police defend society, in his article "The Overlap of Military and Police Responsibilities in Latin America," in the *Journal of Low Intensity Conflict & Law Enforcement* (Autumn 1995). J. Patrice McSherry's "Military Political Power and Guardian Structures in Latin America," in the *Journal of Third World Studies* (Spring 1995), makes the case for enduring and hopelessly predatory militarism in contemporary South America. Despite five pages of footnotes, McSherry's force ratios and structural portrayals are wildly inaccurate.

Your reviewer examined the economic role of those same armed forces in the Fall 1992 issue of *Strategic Review* in an article titled "The role of Latin American Armed Forces in the 1990s." Three other pieces by your reviewer examined the delicate issue of transmitting professional values from US to Latin American military personnel via training programs offered in the Spanish language. These are "Forty Years of Human Rights Training" in the Autumn 1995 issue of the *Journal of Low Intensity Conflict & Law Enforcement*, "U.S. Military Courses for Latin Americans Are a Low-Budget Strategic Success," in *North-South: The Magazine of the Americas* (February-March 1993); and "A

Military Turn of Mind: Educating Latin American Officers," in the August 1993 *Military Review*.

Several new books critique US policy on specific thorn-in-the-side countries. Former Ambassador (to Haiti) Ernest H. Preeg posits a fascinating theory about the relationship of arable land, land tenure, population, and US Haitian policy. His 1996 volume *The Haitian Dilemma* ... was sponsored by the Center for International and Strategic Studies. Joseph S. Tulchin authored and edited with Gary Bland in 1992 the excellent study *Is There a Transition to Democracy in El Salvador?* Tentative optimism at that time required courage, and subsequent events seem to bear out the author-editors' conclusion that a genuine political democracy is slowly emerging in that once war-torn land. Saul Landau gives Uncle Sam a mighty buffet in his 1993 polemic *The Guerrilla Wars of Central America: Nicaragua, El Salvador, and Guatemala*. This book could have been written from the New York Public Library, employing the articles in *Nation* and *The Progressive* as sources; there is hardly any material on guerrilla warfare in it. Stephen C. Benz's *Guatemalan Journey* (1996) displays critical scholarly objectivity, while Victor Perera's *Unfinished Conquest: The Guatemalan Tragedy* (1995) offers a native leftist's views. While indicting the Guatemalan army for human rights abuses, Perera also blames the leftist guerrillas for dragging the indigenous Guatamalans into their bloody and unwinnable struggle.

Your reviewer examined this melancholy literature in an essay called "Reading Up on the Drug War," in *Parameters* (Autumn 1995). Some important new writing has appeared.

Starting close to home, Timothy J. Dunn has produced a 1996 book called *The Militarization of the U.S.-Mexico Border, 19787-1992: Low Intensity Conflict Comes Home*. His work is part of the Border and Migration Studies Series, sponsored by the University of Texas's Center for Mexican-American Studies. Since a heightened US military role in the US-Mexican border scenario is an issue for the November 1996 US presidential election, the importance of this study can hardly be exaggerated. Historian William O. Walker III has written several prominent studies on US drug war policy. Now comes his 1996 *Drugs in the Western Hemisphere*, part of the distinguished Jaguar Series from Scholarly Resources, Inc. This book is simply the best in its field.

A strategy of the drug lords in Colombia for years has been to forge an unholy alliance with the leftist guerrillas; the narco-thugs have the cash, while the guerrillas have manpower, an elegant propaganda machine, and quasi-respectability. Such distinguished entities as Amnesty International and *The New York Times* have been regularly deceived into believing that the Colombian army and National Police, plus a fictitious "right-wing militia," are the perpetrators of human rights violations. Retired Major General Miguel Sanmiguel, a highly decorated human rights hero and military historian, lays bare the defamatory plot in his article "Human Rights Violations in Colombia: Colombian Government and Military Perspectives," in the *Journal of Low Intensity Conflict & Law Enforcement* (Autumn 1995). Sanmiguel's article can be read in its original Spanish in the March-April 1995 "50th Anniversary" issue of *Military Review (Hispanic Edition)*. Easily located opinion surveys in Colombia reveal that public confidence in the Army has never wavered, but great damage has been done internationally when major US news chains allude to the "killings by the Colombian military" as if they were discussing the Salvadoran army or National Guard of 1981.

Cuba and the Far Left

Your reviewer has been making the point for several years that Fidel Castro considers himself to be neither historically idiosyncratic nor erroneous. The 1962 film *El Cid* ended with the hero's cadaver strapped upon his horse in full armor, leading the troops to victory and then being cantered off down the Mediterranean beach into immortality. Charlton Heston played the role of this medieval Spaniard grandly. Fidel Castro, son of a Spanish multimillionaire, is no slouch of an actor, but neither has he any intention of being trotted down the beach into the Caribbean. US Latin American specialists have extolled and fawned over the Castro revolution since late 1960, when Professor Stanely Stein pronounced the death of constitutional democracy in Latin America before the Conference on Latin American History (*Hispanic American Historical Review*, August 1961), yet since Cold War's end they've lined up to predict his imminent downfall. The big question is how to explain his apparent staying power, and several scholars are doing it well.

Enrique A. Baloyra and James A. Morris are author-editors of the 1993 work *Conflict and Change in Cuba*, a multidisciplinary collection of essays which reveal adaptability and toughness within the beleaguered Cuban revolution. Carolee Bengelsdorf shows in his 1994 book, *The Problem of Democracy in Cuba: Vision and Reality*, that Castro has often balanced pragmatism with idealism in order to survive. Frank T. Fitzgerald's 1994 study, *The Cuban Revolution in Crisis: From Managing Socialism to Managing Survival*, makes a similar case from a different perspective. Jorge F. Perez-Lopez offers previously unknown material about recent policy shifts in Havana in his 1994 volume, *Cuba at a Crossroads: Politics and Economics After the Fourth Party Congress*.

The best literary action pertaining to Cuba is easily Mary-Alice Waters' pair of edited volumes containing Ernesto Che Guevara's essays and field notes from the Cuban 1957-1959) and Bolivian (1967) campaigns. Guevara belongs to the select company of revolutionary architects who also commanded in the field, died for the cause, and polarized the forces of history for a generation or more. Waters' book—*The Bolivian Diary of Ernesto Che Guevara* (1994) and *Episodes* of the Cuban Revolutionary War, 1956-68 (1996)—create the same level of literary immortality for the Argentine apostle of neo-Marxism that US Marine Corps General Samuel B. Griffith did for the works of Mao Zedong (Mao Tsetung), and the Roman General Flavius Arrianus did for Alexander the Great. Her two cross-referenced and beautifully annotated volumes belong in all library collections pertaining to Latin America. Your reviewer's "On Castro and Cuba: Rethinking the 'Three Gs,'" in the Autumn 1995 issue of *Parameters* evaluates several more studies and memoirs of importance on the Cuban revolution.

BIBLIOGRAPHY

Baloyrz, Enrique A., and James A. Morris, eds. *Conflict and Change in Cuba.* Albuquerque: Univ. of New Mexico Press, 1993.

Bengelsdorf, Carolee. *The Problem of Democracy in Cuba: Vision and Reality.* New York: Oxford Univ. Press, 1994.

Benz, Stephen Connely. *Guatemalan Journey.* Austin: Univ. of Texas Press, 1996.

Buchanan, Paul G. "U.S. Defense Policy for the Western Hemisphere: New Wine in Old Bottles, Old Wine in New Bottles, or Something Completely Different?" *Journal of Inter-American Studies & World Affairs*, 38 (Spring 1996).

Chaffee, Wilber A., Jr. *The Economics of Violence in Latin America: A Theory of Political Competition.* Westport, Conn.: Greenwood Publishing Group, 1992.

Clarke, Walter S., and Arthur E. Dewey. "Peace/Humanitarian Operations: Introducing the 'Comprehensive Campaign Plan.'" Occasional Paper, US Southern Command & Congressional Hunger Center, 1996.

Demarest, Geoffrey B. "The Overlap of Military and Police Responsibilities in Latin America," *Journal of Low Intensity Conflict & Law Enforcement*, 4 (Autumn 1995).

Dent, David W., ed. *U.S.-Latin American Policymaking: A Reference Handbook.* Westport, Conn.: Greenwood, 1995.

Dostert, Pierre Etienne. *Latin America 1996.* The World Today Series. Rpt.; Harpers Ferry, W. Va.: Stryker-Post Publications, 1996.

Dunn, Timothy J. *The Militarization of the U.S.-Mexico Border, 1978-1999: Low Intensity Conflict Comes Home.* Center for Mexican-American Studies, "Border & Migration Studies" Series. Austin: Univ. of Texas Press, 1996.

Einaudi, Luigi, ed. *Beyond Cuba: Latin America Takes Charge of Its Future.* The RAND Corporation. New York: Crane Russak, 1974. Out of print.

Fitzgerald, Frank T. *The Cuban Revolution in Crisis: From Managing Socialism to Managing Survival.* New York: Monthly Review Press, 1994.

Gross, Liza. *Handbook of Leftist Guerrilla Groups in Latin America and the Caribbean*. Boulder, Colo.: Westview Press, 1995.

Keen, Benjamin, ed. *Latin American Civilization: History and Society, 1492 to the Present*. Rpt.; Boulder, Colo.: Westview Press, 1996.

Landau, Saul. *The Guerrilla Wars of Central America: Nicaragua, El Salvador, and Guatemala*. New York: St. Martin's Press, 1993.

Lowenthal, Abraham F., and Gregory F. Treverton, eds. *Latin America in a New World*. Inter-American Dialogue Series. Boulder, Colo.: Westview Press, 1994.

MacDonald, Scott B., et al. *Fast Forward: Latin America on the Edge of the Twenty-First Century*. Center for Strategic and International Studies. New Brunswick, N.J.: Transaction, 1996.

Martz, John D., ed. *United States Policy in Latin America*. Lincoln: Univ. of Nebraska Press, 1995.

McSherry, J. Patrica. "Military Political Power and Guardian Structures in Latin America," *Journal of Third World Studies*, 12 (Spring 1995).

Mirandz, Roger, and William Ratliff. *The Civil War in Nicaragua: Inside the Sandinistas*. Rpt.; New Brunswick, N.J.: Rutgers Univ. Press, 1993.

O'Brien, Raymond M. "Regional Security in Latin America: U.S. Economic and Military Options," *Strategic Review*, 20 (Fall 1992).

Pererz, Victor. *Unfinished Conquest: The Guatemalan Tragedy*. Berkeley: Univ., of California Press, 1995.

Perez-Lopez, Jorge F. *Cuba at a Crossroads: Politics and Economics After the Fourth Party Congress*. Gainesville: Univ. of Florida Press, 1994.

Preeg, Ernest H. *The Haitian Dilemma: A Case Study in Demographics, Development, and U.S. Foreign Policy*. Center for Strategic and International Studies, "Significant Issues" Series. Washington: CSIS Press, 1996.

Ramsey, Russell W. "Forty Years of Human Rights Training." *Journal of Low Intensity Conflict & Law Enforcement*, 4 (Autumn 1995).

_____. "Hopeful Neoliberals, Derailed Collectivists—Emerging Paradigms on Latin America." *Journal of Comparative Strategy,* 14 (Winter 1996*).*

_____. "Latin American Military Affairs." *Military Review*, 76 (March-April 1996).

_____. "A Military Turn of Mind: Educating Latin American Officers." *Military Review*, 73 (Aug. 1993).

_____. "On Castro and Cuba: Rethinking the 'Three Gs.'" *Parameters*, 24 (Winter 1994-95).

_____. "Reading Up on the Drug War." *Parameters*, 25 (Autumn 1995).

_____. "The Role of Latin American Armed Forces in the 1990s." *Strategic Review*, 20 (Fall 1992).

_____. "Strategic Reading on Latin America." *Parameters*, 24 (Summer 1994).

_____. "Strategic Reading on Latin America: 1995 Update." *Parameters*, 25 (Winter 1995-956).

_____. "U.S. Military Courses for Latin Americans Are a Low-Budget Strategic Success." *North-South: The Magazine of the Americas*, 2 (February-March 1993).

_____. "US Strategy for Latin America." *Parameters*, 24 (Autumn 1994).

Sanmiguel Buenaventura, Manuel. "Human Rights Violations in Colombia: Colombian Government and Military Perspectives." *Journal of Low Intensity Conflict & Law Enforcement*, 4 (Autumn 1995).

Sheinin, David. *The Organization of American States*. International Organizations Series, Vol. II. New Brunswick, N.J.: Transaction, 1995.

Swatos, William H., ed. *Religion and Democracy in Latin America*. New Brunswick, N.J.: Transaction, 1995.

Tulchin, Joseph S., ed, with Gary Bland. *Is There a Transition to Democracy in El Salvador?* Boulder, Colo.: Lynne Rienner, 1992.

Walker, William O., III. *Drugs in the Western Hemisphere*. The Jaguar Series. Wilmington: Scholarly Resources, 1996.

Waters, Mary-Allice, ed. *The Bolivian Diary of Ernesto Che Guevara*. New York Pathfinder Pres, 1994.

_____. Ed. *Episodes of the Cuban Revolutionary War, 1956-58*. New York Pathfinder Press, 1996.

Wiarda, Howard J. "After Miami: The summit Crisis, the Peso Crisis, and the Future of U.S.-Latin American Relations." *Journal of Interamerican Studies and World Affairs*, 37 (Spring 1995).

Wiarda, Howard J. *Democracy and Its Discontents: Development, Interdependence, and U.S. Policy in Latin America*. Lanham, Md.: Rowman & Littlefield, 1995.

The Reviewer: Russell W. Ramsey is a civilian professor at the US Army School of the Americas. He holds the Ph.D. degree in Latin American history from the University of Florida and has written many articles and books on Latin American military topics.

Analysis of the US-Mexican Border:
A Strategic Literature Yet to Come
Parameters Autumn 1997
RUSSELL W. RAMSEY

© 1997 Russell W. Ramsey

The US national security community bases its policies and strategies on the legitimacy of sovereignty, the philosophical centerpiece of the nation-state since the 1648 Treaty of Westphalia. The national security planner and the strategist who would visualize the massive flow of illegal immigration and the related narcotrafficking problem at the US border with Mexico through the eyes of the contemporary strategic literature is in for a rude surprise. The US-Mexican border literature is not strategic in nature; it is little more than an inventory of problems.

Ambassador George Kennan's 1947 "Mr. 'X'" article in *Foreign Affairs* sounded the national security tocsin, to the satisfaction of most thinking people in the Judeo-Christian West, producing a robust, legitimate, and ultimately winning defense against the neo-barbarians of the communist East. Central to the policy of containment and the strategy of deterrence against communism were the value and legitimacy of the nation-state. By viewing the US-Mexican border as a giant social problem instead of a legitimate national security issue, the scholarly community is simply not producing a serious analysis of what is, essentially, a strategic set of issues involving sovereignty, borders, and the future of two huge nation-states.

Caspar Weinberger, Secretary of Defense from 1981 to 1987, has penned a novel with an obvious political message. Called *The Next War*, his 1996 chiller depicts five scenarios that project the United States into large-scale armed conflict. In one scenario, the United States invades Mexico in response to runaway illegal immigration, northward flow of illegal drugs, rampant corruption, and seemingly uncontrollable political terrorism. The Mexican government is presented as completely incompetent to operate a stable political democracy, a veritable band of thugs in complicity with the worst criminal elements. If Weinberger's book was meant to be a caveat to Mexican government officials, the effect is unfortunate, for the scenario played out in the book fuels the ultraconservative myth that there are no functional strategic solutions to the problem short of outright invasion. Mexicans in 1997 have not forgotten the US occupation of Veracruz harbor in 1914 and the Pershing invasion expedition two years later.

If the Weinberger book reaches too fast for the trigger on the US-Mexican border problem, one might consult Timothy J. Dunn's 1996 study, *The Militarization of the U.S.-Mexico Border, 1978-1992.* Dunn offers an important inventory of cooperation among local, state, and federal law enforcement agencies across the southwestern United States in their efforts to check the flow of illegal northward immigration. Then he creates a theory by summing up four national security issues affecting Latin America in the recent past: cooperative security measures on the US-Mexican border; the drug war, which he considers fictitious or pretextual; US policy in Central America during the 1980s, central to today's wave of democratization; and opposition to Fidel Castro's military adventurism. For Dunn, these prove the existence of a militaristic Anglo-Saxon conspiracy against Latin America.

Professor Wayne A. Cornelius of the University of California at San Diego has assembled an unusually comprehensive set of essays on immigration policy. His 1994 edited volume *Controlling Immigration: A Global Perspective* discovers a "convergence hypothesis" among the industrially developed countries who import cheap labor from developing nations. But he also validates a "gap hypothesis," meaning that, as these converging policies continue in place, they increasingly fail to accomplish their stated purpose, namely, to impose limits on an unwanted flood of economic immigrants. Professor Cornelius's conclusions were presented in his superb essay called "Economics, Culture, and the Politics of Restricting Immigration" in the 15 November 1996 issue of the *Chronicle of Higher Education.* He calls for the nation-states affected by economic immigration to establish some fundamental parameters, to decide what it is that they really want to do when they invite cheap foreign labor to immigrate and then take measures to restrict the ensuing ethnic flood.

The literature on illegal economic immigration, then, is either highly politicized on the liberal-conservative spectrum or narrow in scope. One suspects that professor sin fields like agricultural economics and international finance will seize the torch on such critical issues as illegal immigration across the border between the United States and Mexico, given that these specialists are already creating a good literature on privatization and democratization in Latin America. The 1996 Index issue of the *Latin American Research Review*, which is the nation's prime source of research interest by scholars specializing in Latin America, shows only six articles dedicated to the Mexican border problem in 25 years. Scholars of international relations, national security policy, and military strategy need to revitalize the meaning of sovereignty in the milieu of massively penetrated borders.

BIBLIOGRAPHY

Cornelius, Wayne, et al., eds. *Controlling Immigration: A Global Perspective.* Palo Alto, Calif.: Stanford Univ. Press, 1994.

_____. "Economics, Culture, and the Politics of Restricting Immigration," *Chronicle of Higher Education*, 15 November 1996.

Dunn, Timothy J. *The Militarization of the U.S. Mexico Border 1978-1992.* Austin: Univ. of Texas Press, 1996.

Weinberger, Caspar, and Peter Schweizer. *The Next War.* Washington: Regnery Publishers, 1996.

The Reviewer: Russell W. Ramsey is a civilian professor at the US Army School of the Americas. He holds the Ph.D. degree in Latin American history from the University of Florida and has written many articles and books on Latin American military topics.

Russell W. Ramsey, Ph.D., D.Min.

Strategic Reading on Latin America
1998 Update
<u>Parameters</u> Spring 1998
RUSSELL W. RAMSEY

The entries in this fourth annual appraisal of the strategic literature pertaining to Latin America are presented in six categories, all of which have some degree of overlap. Three themes previously established in this review essay series continue here. The first is that the post-Cold War era offers a disparate set of regional strategic challenges. The second is that Latin America is moving solidly along the twin trajectories of democratic pluralization and neo-liberal economic development, despite a lingering neo-Marxist and frequently pessimistic mind-set among US academic specialists on Latin America. The third is the ironic fact that despite the first two trends, strategic assessments of Latin America are of decisively better quality than comparable studies written during the Cold War.

Political and Philosophical Issues

Charles D. Brockett and a team of southeastern US Latin Americanists produced a Reserve Officers Association National Security Report called "Latin America in Transition: Politics and Democracy." Excerpted from a longer study, the piece is a superb strategic introduction to the region for professional and academic readership alike. Latin America specialists in the Atlanta region have cooperated with business leaders to create the Southern Center for International Studies, and the paper by Brockett et al. is the introduction from a textbook bearing the same title. A full agenda of regional challenges prevents rose-tinted optimism from dominating the text. Jorge I. Dominguez invokes the Latin American political buzzword *fracasomania* (translates loosely as "obsession with the idea that things are politically chaotic") as the theme for his essay "Latin America's Crisis of Representation," which cautions against excessive political optimism. Lawrence E. Harrison relies on the old "Pan-American dream" for a book title; he examines a 125-year-old regional paradigm for economic cooperation in the post-Cold War context. Since President Benjamin Harrison's support for the conference series that became the Pan-American Union in 1889, the United States has periodically spearheaded campaigns to nurture a neo-liberal economic system in the Western Hemisphere. Lawrence Harrison gives the post-Cold War regional privatization and tariff reduction movement an important historical rung on this ladder.

Elizabeth Jelin and Eric Hershberg offer a set of essays that examine the key aspects of regional democratization in their book *Constructing Democracy: Human Rights, Citizenship, and Society in Latin America.* They represent a viewpoint often expressed by nongovernmental actors on a reformist mission. Eldon Kenworthy identifies excessive focus upon sovereignty as a limiting force in *America/Americas: Myth in the Making of U.S. Policy Toward Latin America.* Paul H. Lewis fires a powerful salvo against neo-Marxist bias among US Latin American political science specialists in his "Review Essay: Political Scholarship." Professor Lewis believes that Latin Americanists in the United States rejected the optimistic worldview prevalent in the early 1960s as pseudo-scientific. They dumped this neo-positivistic outlook for an even more distorted outlook, Ernesto "Che" Guevara's neo-Marxism, which prescribes armed revolution and one-party dictatorship for all of Latin America. Scott B. MacDonald and Georges A. Fauriol offer detailed analysis of seven important Latin American countries in *Fast Forward: Latin American on the Edge of the 21st Century.*

Military Activities

A literature generally less emotional and less politically biased has emerged on this topic. Tom Farer provides an excellent set of essays in his book *Beyond Sovereignty: Collectively Defending Democracy in the Americas.* Professor Farer correctly identifies sovereignty as the value that defines the approach that Latin American nations have taken to the inter-American system. Since the Cold War's end, he opines, the United States must grant a larger, more sovereign role to the "other Americas" if there is to be an effective system of regional security. John T. Fishel's *Civil Military Operations in the New World* analyzes hemispheric use of military forces for operations other than war. Examples drawn from both north and south allow a comparison of Latin America with other, more turbulent world regions. Fishel has also coauthored with Iimbra L. Fishel the monograph "The Impact of an Educational Institution on Host Nation Militaries," a sophisticated rationale for sustaining the US Army School of the Americas as an instrument of US military policy, and revealing the human rights protest to be a disguise for deeper political agendas. Joseph C. Leuer's "School of the Americas and U.S. Foreign Policy Attainment in Latin America" covers much of the same ground by matching the school's curriculum against foreign policy goals of the Clinton Administration.

Michael Klare and David Anderson suggest in *A Scourge of Guns: The Diffusion of Small Arms and Light Weapons in Latin America* that all social sectors within the region are inundated by easily accessible small arms. Their solutions are the statutory limitation of arms importation and a vast reduction in military forces, which are already the smallest per capita (save in Cuba) among the world's regions.

Brian Loveman and Thomas M. Davies, Jr., have updated their collection of essays called *The Politics of Anti-politics: The Military in Latin America*. The central thesis remains: Latin American military leaders claim their governmental takeovers to be politically neutral stewardship regimes, while in fact these regimes generate their own negative politics. The essays are outdated, even if updated. Richard L. Millett and Michael Gold-Biss, by contrast, have edited what promises to be the most significant book on Latin American military forces in three decades. Called *Beyond Praetorianism: The Latin American Military in Transition*, the title is self explanatory, and the tone is guardedly optimistic. The volume includes essays by a balanced group of analysts skilled and experienced in civil-military relationships in Latin America. Emerging roles, force structures, and police-military relationships are analyzed, as is the ever emotional topic of US security assistance and its linkage to human rights issues.

Your reviewer recently published *Guardians of the Other Americas: Essays on the Military Forces of Latin America*; the real value of the essays lies in nothing the date of original publication and the context. Glenn R. Weidner and a group of writers offer "United States Military Group-Honduras: Supporting Democracy in Central America" in *The DISAM Journal of International Security Assistance Management*. Weidner played an important role in negotiating a truce during the recent Ecuador-Peru border flare-up. *The DISAM Journal*, in which Weidner's article appears, represents the only effort by a country operating an international security assistance program to make that program fully known in costs, staffing, weapons and equipment, training, and rationale, thus negating the oft-expressed neo-Marxist claim that US security assistance is a secret and sinister affair.

Drug War

Sewall H. Menzel's *Fire in the Andes: U.S. Foreign Policy and Cocaine Politics in Bolivia and Peru* is an insider's powerful argument that only by significantly reducing demand for narcotics in the United States can the drug war be won in the Andean region. Menzel's companion volume *Cocaine Quagmire: Implementing the U.S. Anti-Drug Policy in the North Andes-Colombia* is the best work to date on this topic. The final chapter should be mandatory reading for all US national security community personnel who work on or want to understand the Andean drug war scene. Menzel examines supply-side and demand-side arguments and shows how the shower of drug money arriving in Colombia from the United States has corrupted a previously model political system, leaving the army and national police to fight on alone at the cost of over 300 combat casualties per year. Luis Alberto Villamarin Pulido's translated revelation *The FARC Cartel* lays bare the marriage of two evil empires, the leftist "FARC" guerrillas of Colombia and the former drug carters. North Americans who read this honest account may fee remorse over the distortions about the Colombian drug war regularly produced by such distinguished sources as *The New York Times*, *The Washington Post*, and National Public Radio. Your reviewer's bibliographic essay on this melancholy topic appeared in *Parameters* (Autumn 1995).

Indigenous Peoples

Hector Diaz Polanco has authored the excellent book, *Indigenous Peoples in Latin America: The Quest for Self-Determination*; while several trapped minority populations have a potential for national security concerns, the Latin American region is vastly better off than, say, the Balkans, Cyprus, Rwanda and Burundi, or Northern Ireland. Donna Lee Van Cott's *Defiant Again: Indigenous Peoples and Latin American Security* is an example and trenchantly worded analysis of this topic. Von Cott's work shows how Latin America's long history of tolerance for its ethnic minorities has nevertheless left the minorities largely outside the economic growth of past decades. Druglords and Marxist guerrillas will continue to arm the unlanded minorities against their governments, she concludes, until an equitable land tenure and market participation formula is found for each ethnic group.

Economics

Thomas J. Desrosier's monograph "Neo-Liberal Economics and the Latin American Military," which relates military roles to economic development, is based upon a survey of mid-career Latin American officers. The 5th LATAM Conference at the US Army School of the Americas in 1995 offered a dozen guest lectures by experts on this topic, and a summarized "Conference Proceedings" was published.

Sandor Halebsky and Richard L. Harris have edited *Capital, Power, and Inequality in Latin America*. The authors included are generally skeptical that neo-liberal economics are anything but one more scheme by which the rich despoil the poor in Latin America. Ricardo Hausmann and Liliana Rojas-Suarez have written a short and somewhat technical book, *Banking Crisis in Latin America*, which should be read alongside recent articles in *The London Economist* on the same topic for a fuller and more balanced view of events.

Paul Craig Roberts and Karen LaFollette Araujo offer a technically impressive, if somewhat dubious, critique in *The Capitalist Revolution in Latin America.* Their data allow the reader to make a full evaluation of Latin America's current privatization movement. While the authors do not seem to advocate a return to state-owned enterprises, or to a neo-Marxist system, they show clearly that capitalism in Latin American societies has always exacted a price in human suffering. Thomas E. Skidmore and Peter H. Smith offer the third edition of their introductory textbook *Modern Latin America*, with a heavily negative economic view of the post-Cold War era. Jeffrey Stark's monograph entitled "Health" in the University of Miami's *North-South Issues* series is a good survey of a critical issue, as is his "Sustainable Development," in the same series.

Specific Countries and Sub-Regions

Roderic Al Camp is a highly regarded specialist on the Mexican military institution. His *Politics in Mexico* is fundamental reading on that rapidly changing milieu. Professor Camp is also the author of important studies on Mexican military officer behavior and values. As the *Partido Revolucionario Institucionalizado* (PRI) loses its one-party power grip, its 75-year span of control over the officer corps is a collateral casualty. A new civil-military paradigm emerges, just as the drug war projects the Mexican Army into new internal roles. T. R. Ferenbach's *Fire and Blood: A History of Mexico* presents the country as a historical cauldron of unresolved social conflicts. Gerardo Otero's collection of essays entitled *Neoliberalism Revisited: Economic Restructuring and Mexico's Political Future* is fundamental strategic reading.

Alex Dupuy's *Haiti in the New World Order* rests on the highly debatable viewpoint that US imperialism created Haiti's endemic problem with repressive military and police institutions. Ivelaw L. Griffith offers an excellent strategic analysis in the monograph *Caribbean Security on the Eve of the 21st Century.* Griffith teamed up with Betty N. Sedoc-Dahlberg to edit *Democracy and Human Rights in the Caribbean*, a reasonably balanced treatment of the subject. Lester D. Langley and Thomas Schoonover offer *The Banana Men: American Mercenaries & Entrepreneurism in Central America, 1880-1930*, which explores the political and commercial side of the banana diplomacy era in that region. Their work seems intended to complement Ivan Musicant's *The Banana War: A History of United States Military Intervention in Latin America from the Spanish-American War to the Invasion of Panama.* J. Patrice McSherry's *Incomplete Transition: Military Power and Democracy in Argentina* reveals a fundamental dislike of Argentina's military institutions, so strong that no amount of reform will satisfy the author. The evidence offered in support of her dismal conclusions is thin, negatively selective, and outdated. Tommie Sue Montgomery's article "Constructing Democracy in El Salvador" is the best analysis yet on this emotion-laden topic.

Louis A. Perez, Jr., authored *Cuba: Between Reform and Revolution*. The title is self-explanatory, and the book helps explain Fidel Castro's remarkable capacity to remain in power. Marifeli Perez-Stable's *The Cuban Revolution: Origins, Course, and Legacy* is but one of many interpretive works on a topic that seems to fascinate authors.

Nazih Richani's "The Political Economy of Violence" The War System in Colombia," is based on limited evidence. The article reaches the remarkable conclusion that the Colombian armed forces, presently losing about 300 soldiers annually in combat with narco-terrorists, are part of a giant interest group conspiracy to keep the drug war afloat because it provides good salaries.

BIBLIOGRAPHY

Brockett, Charles D., et al. "Latin America in Transition: Politics and Democracy." Excerpt from text by Southern Center for International Studies/ROA National Security Report, *The Officer*, November 1996, pp. 31-34, 38.

Camp, Roderic Al. *Politics in Mexico*. New York: Oxford Univ. Press, 1993.

Desrosier, Thomas J. "Neo-Liberal Economics and the Latin American Military." Occasional paper, Troy State University, June 1997.

Diaz Polanco, Hector. *Indigenous Peoples in Latin America: The Quest for Self-Determination*. Latin American Perspective Series, No. 18. Trans. Lucia Rayas. Boulder, Colo.: Westview Press, 1997.

Dominguez, Jorge I. "Latin America's Crisis of Representation." *Foreign Affairs*, 76 (January-February 1997), 100-13.

Dupuy, Alex. *Haiti in the New World Order*. Boulder, Colo.: Westview Press, 1997.

Farer, Tom, ed. *Beyond Sovereignty: Collectively Defending Democracy in the Americas*. Baltimore: Johns Hopkins Univ. Press, 1996.

Ferenbach, T. R. *Fire and Blood: A History of Mexico*. New York: Da Capo Press, 1995.

Fishel, John T. *Civil Military Operations in the New World*. Westport, Conn.: Greenwood, 1997.

Fishel, John T., and Kimbra L. Fishel. "The Impact of an Educational Institution on Host Nation Militaries." Monograph, Ft. Leavenworth, Kans., 1996.

Griffith, Ivelaw L. *Caribbean Security on the Eve of the 21st Century*. Institute for National Strategic Studies, McNair Paper #54. Washington: National Defense Univ., 1996.

Griffith, Ivelaw L., and Betty N. Sedoc-Dahlberg, eds. *Democracy and Human Rights in the Caribbean*. Boulder, Colo.: Westview Press, 1997.

Halebsky, Sandor, and Richard L. Harris, eds. *Capital, Power, and Inequality in Latin America*. Boulder, Colo.: Westview Press, 1995.

Harrison, Lawrence E. *The Pan-American Dream*. New York: Basic Books, 1997.

Hausmann, Ricardo, and Liliana Rojas-Suarez. *Banking Crisis in Latin America*. Washington: Inter-American Development Bank, 1996.

Jelin, Elizabeth, and Eric Hershberg, eds. *Constructing Democracy: Human Rights, Citizenship, and Society in Latin America*. Boulder, Colo.: Westview Press, 1996.

Kenworthy, Eldon. *America/Americas: Myth in the Making of U.S. Policy Toward Latin America*. University Park: Pennsylvania State Univ. Press, 1995.

Klare, Michael, and David Anderson. *A Scourge of Guns: The Diffusion of Small Arms and Light Weapons in Latin America*. Washington: Federation of American Scientists/Arms Sales Monitoring Project, 1996.

Langley, Lester D., and Thomas Schoonover. *The Banana Men: American Mercenaries & Enterpreneurism in Central America 1880-1930*. Lexington: Univ. of Kentucky Press, 1995.

Leuer, Joseph C. "School of the Americas and U.S. Foreign Policy Attainment in Latin America." Monograph, Ft. Benning, Ga., 1996.

Lewis, Paul H. "Review Essay: Political Scholarship." *Journal of Interamerican Studies & World Affairs*, 38 (Winter 1996), 193-200.

Loveman, Brian, and Thomas M. Davies, Jr., eds. *The Politics of Anti-politics: The Military in Latin America*. Wilmington, Del.: Scholarly Resources, 1997.

MacDonald, Scott B., and Georges A. Fauriol. *Fast Forward: Latin America on the Edge of the 21st Century*. New Brunswick, N.J.: Transaction Publishers, 1997.

McSherry, J. Patrice. *Incomplete Transition: Military Power and Democracy in Argentina*. New York: St. Martin's Press, 1997.

Menzel, Sewall H. *Cocaine Quagmire: Implementing the U.S. Anti-Drug Policy in the North Andes-Colombia*. Lanham, Md.: Univ. Press of America, 1997.

_____. *Fire in the Andes: U.S. Foreign Policy and Cocaine Politics in Bolivia and Peru*. Lanham, Md.: Univ. Press of America, 1996.

Millett, Richard L., and Michael Gold-Biss, eds. *Beyond Praetorianism: The Latin American Military in Transition*. Coral Gables, Fla.: North-South Center/Univ. of Miami Press, 1996.

Montgomery, Tommie Sue. "Constructing Democracy in El Salvador," *Current History*, 96 (February 1997), 61-68.

Musitant, Ivan. *The Banana Wars: A History of United States Military Intervention in Latin America from the Spanish-American War to the Invasion of Panama*. New York: Macmillan, 1990.

Otero, Gerardo, ed. *Neoliberalism Revisited: Economic Restructuring and Mexico's Political Future*. Boulder, Colo.: Westview Press, 1996.

Perez, Louis A., Jr. *Cuba: Between Reform and Revolution*. 2d ed. New York: Oxford Univ. Press, 1995.

Perez-Stable, Marifeli. *The Cuban Revolution: Origins, Course, and Legacy*. New York: Oxford Univ. Press, 1993.

Ramsey, Russell W. *Guardians of the Other Americas: Essays on the Military Forces of Latin America*. Lanham, Md.: Univ. Press of America, 1997.

Richani, Nazih. "The Political Economy of Violence: The War System in Colombia," *Journal of Interamerican Studies & World Affairs*, 39 (Summer 1997), 37-82.

Roberts, Paul Craig, and Karen LaFollette Araujo. *The Capitalist Revolution in Latin America*. New York: Oxford Univ. Press, 1997.

Skidmore, Thomas E., and Peter H. Smith. *Modern Latin America*. 3d ed. New York, Oxford Univ. Press, 1992.

Stark, Jeffrey. *North-South Issues: Health*, 6 (No. 1, 1997).

_____. *North-South Issues: Sustainable Development*, 6 (No. 2, 1997).

Van Cott, Donna Lee. *Defiant Again: Indigenous Peoples and Latin American Security*. Institute for National Strategic Studies, McNair Paper #53. Washington: National Defense Univ., 1996.

Villamarin Pulido, Luis Alberto. *The FARC Cartel*. Trans. Alfredo de Zubiria Meriano. Bogota: Ediciones "El Faraon," 1996.

Weidner, Glenn R., et al., "United States Military Group-Honduras; Supporting Democracy in Central America," *The DISAM Journal of International Security Assistance Management*, 18 (Summer 1996), 1-34.

The Reviewer: Russell W. Ramsey is a civilian professor at the US Army School of the Americas. He holds the Ph.D. degree in Latin American history from the University of Florida and has written many articles and book on Latin American military topics.

Latin America: A Booming Strategic Region
In Need of an Honest Introductory Textbook
<u>Parameters</u> Spring 1998
RUSSELL W. RAMSEY

According to the Administration's *A National Security Strategy for a New Century* (May 1997), "Our hemisphere enters the twenty-first century with an unprecedented opportunity to build a future of stability and prosperity—building on the fact that every nation in the hemisphere except Cuba is democratic and committed to free market economies." Yet two textbooks commonly used for introductory college courses on Latin America present the region in 1998 as a revolutionary cauldron where democracy is a sham, and where the people are pauperized by greedy US corporations and often murdered by huge US-trained armies. This fifth annual *Parameters* essay on the strategic literature on Latin America will examine the question of ideological interpretation.

Regional Surveys and References

Robert T. Buckman's *Latin America, 1998* is the 32d annual entry into the Latin American field by the distinguished Stryker-Post series on world regions. It is packed with detail, yet readable; philosophically ample, yet focused; historically rooted, yet very contemporary. These factors, plus its inexpensive paperback format, make Buckman's volume the regional survey of choice. Simon Collier, Thomas E. Skidmore, and the late Harold Blakemore edited the 2d edition of *The Cambridge Encyclopedia of Latin America and the Caribbean* in 1992. Neither a text nor a reference encyclopedia, this costly hardback follows the topical commentary format pioneered by the French encyclopedist Denis Diderot in the 1750s. It is therefore neither a complete reference tool nor a purely factual commentary, innocent of ideological slant. The Europa Publisher, Brassey's Ltd., and the International Institute for Strategic Studies, all of London, publish annually updated reference volumes that better accomplish the regional strategic reference task.

Regional Histories and Interpretations

Thomas E. Skidmore is a well-established Latin American historian and, coincidentally, a coeditor of the *Cambridge Encyclopedia* just mentioned. His article "Studying the History of Latin America: A Case of Hemispheric

Convergence," in the Winter 1998 issue of *Latin American Research Review*, is a long-needed contribution. Skidmore's title reflects his conclusion that the bitterly divisive historiographical wars of the 1960s have faded, and so they have. Yet Skidmore makes a fascinating case for a newer and richer fabric in the post-Cold War era. Benjamin Keen is one of the grand old men of Latin American history. The 6th edition of his edited *Latin American Civilization: History & Society, 1492 to the Present* (1196) has long since replaced *A History of Latin America from the Beginnings to the Present* (3d edition, 1968), by the late Hubert Herring, as the North American college student's standard introductory textbook. Contents up to 1947 emphasize social history and conflict issues, with reason and balance. Thereafter, Keen abandons his scholarly stance and includes nothing but paeans to socialism, a political and economic option which clearly was rejected within Latin America by 1996. The reader not only gets an artificially inflated view of socialism's legitimacy in the region, but also is left with a void about what everyone else was thinking and doing during the Cold War.

James D. Cockcroft's 1997 volume, *Latin America: History, Politics, and U.S. Policy* (2d edition), is a costly paperback that will pass as an academic textbook for many in an era when the lines between adversarial journalism and scholarly appraisal have been blurred. Should this be the only text used by college students in an introductory course on Latin America, however, those students will be taught, under the guise of academic legitimacy, a large number of explicit falsehoods about Latin America, the United States, and the relationships between the two bodies. Cockcroft uses a standard format by which to pass off his spin-doctored commentary. Each topical portion uses selected historical strands to show the need for bloody socioeconomic revolutions to remedy centuries of injustice. Then comes a descriptive portion showing the local Marxists as the only people who understand the public and have any support. Finally, there is a de rigueur passage which villainizes US regional policy in regard to each topic, showing how Wall Street, the Pentagon, and the oligarchs who govern the United States conspire with evil *latino* power figures to abuse nearly everyone.

Splendid fiction, this material: authors who blame all troubles in Latin America on US Cold Warriors leap quickly from the cognitive to the affective, thence to the realm of entertainment. Some of the sophomores may actually read it. An intellectual explanation for the apparent popularity of this neo-Marxist fantasy, ten years after its universal rejection at the grass roots throughout Latin America, is the object of your reviewer's 1997 article "Neo-Marxism Rides the Black Legend." Only by accepting that the people of Latin America are so functionally inept as to be historically dominated by their own entrepreneurs, generals, and politicians could anyone conclude that the region needs US Marxists to ride to its rescue with revolutionary cadres and a Utopian formula.

Political and Economic Studies

How is democratization faring in the wake of global neo-liberal economics within Latin America? Howard J. Wiarda and Harvey F. Kline have edited the 4th edition (1996) of their volume *Latin American Politics and Development* to reflect the massive post-Cold War changes. For the national security analyst, strategist, or graduate student, this is the volume of choice. Wiarda and Kline are political scientists, but they amply build in the sweeping effects of the global neo-liberal economic movement and its political influence on Latin America. A splendid complement is the 1995 volume by Scott Mainwaring and Timothy R. Scully, *Building Democratic Institutions: Party Systems in Latin America.* These authors show how emerging Latin American political parties are moving from a single-issue orientation (borrowed from French models) to the inclusive "party as a tent" model seen in the United States. Finally, Ernest Bartell and Leigh A. Payne edited *Business and Democracy in Latin American* in 1995, showing how the giddily optimistic "trickle-down" prescriptions and predictions failed partially in the 1980s, but also how the enhanced base of entrepreneurship has indeed produced a broader set of political constituencies.

Civil-Military Issues

Brian Loveman wrote *The Constitution of Tyranny: Regimes of Exception in Spanish America* in 1993, an important reinterpretation of early national Latin America. He shows how the 19th-century elected administrations often gave way to "regimes of exception," which were usually dictatorships by military-looking *caudillo* figures. Accurate history it is, but Loveman's nonrecognition of the same slow and irregular departure of authoritarian regimes in Europe, Asia, Africa, and the Middle East once again resurrects the old Black Legend, namely that Latin Americans manifest a unique preference for flag-waving pseudo-generals on horseback as chief executives.

David R. Mares corrects Loveman's otherwise valuable historical analysis with his 1998 edited volume of essays, *Civil-Military Relations: Building Democracy and Regional Security in Latin America, Southern Asia, and Central Europe.* These cross-cultural essays leave little doubt that militarism is not the dominant issue when developing countries with weak democratic traditions occasionally vest political leadership in their armed forces. Further, the Latin American region comes off as problematic but rapidly improving in this regard, not nearly so likely as other world regions to call out for the men-at-arms in times of political turmoil.

Jorge I. Dominguez's edited book of essays, *International Security & Democracy: Latin America and the Caribbean in the Post-Cold War Era*, makes no attempt to set a single paradigm. But the quality of the writers whose essays comprise this book make it a classic: Caesar D. Sereseres on Central America, Carlos Escude and Andres Fontana on Argentina, and Ivelaw L. Griffith on regional security collaboration all provide blue-chip contributions. Dominguez concludes his summary essay with a recommendation that the United States needs to recognize the external missions of the Latin American armed forces and legitimize these roles through professional help, a sermon your reviewer has preached for many years without many amens from the congregation. In this regard, my 1997 book *Guardians of the Other Americas: Essays on the Military Forces of Latin America* details the efforts of the US Army to help the Latin Americans give up their periodic dependency on military strongmen during the worst of all possible times, the defense against Soviet-Cuban subversion directed against their governments.

Donald E. Schulz's 1998 volume *The Role of the Armed Forces in the Americas: Civil-Military Relations for the 21st Century* is an update on the search for new missions as the Latin Americans shift toward the *posse comitatus* principle of civil-military relations. Glenn R. Weidner's paper titled "Overcoming the Power Gap: Reorienting the Inter-American System for Hemispheric Security" (1998) traces and analyzes the quest for a functional regional security apparatus. Weidner, who was involved in conflict prevention during the 1994 Peru-Ecuador border dispute, concludes that old scars, internal and external, tend to prevent the political support that could yield a world model for conflict prevention.

Social Movements and Revolution

Sonia E. Alverez, Evelina Dagnino, and Arturo Escobar examine several of Latin America's indigenous peoples and the effects of globalizing economics upon them. Their *Cultures of Politics, Politics of Cultures: Re-visioning Latin American Social Movements* (1998) is a collection of essays by anthropologists from both Latin America and the United States. During the Cold War, Fidel Castro planted Cuban cadres within several Latin American ethnic minority regions with the mission of fomenting revolutionary conflict. Post-Cold War Latin America has seen the continuation of some of these struggles, featuring both domestic and external leadership and support. The Alvarez et al. volume is therefore important strategic reading. Its essays confirm two points. First, the neo-liberal economic movement is not enriching Latin America's ethnically distinct regions very much. Second, there is authentic leadership within the nonassimilated regions that is working to adapt old customs and dreams to economic modernity, while sacrificing neither ethnic honor nor authenticity.

Ofelia Schutte's 1993 study *Cultural Identity and Social Liberation in Latin American Thought* reached similar conclusions. Ways must be found, she concluded, to preserve the ethnic dignity and authenticity of old submerged cultures, even as those same cultures must learn to accept some aspects of modernity in order to enjoy its economic and technological advantages. Finally, Cynthia McClintock's *Revolutionary Movements in Latin America: El Salavador's FMLN and Peru's Shining Path* (1998) achieves two goals. It is the latest and best interpretation of El Salvador's 1980s civil war and of Peru's long struggle to contain the Shining Path movement. Additionally, McClintock sets a new standard of scholarly excellence for this kind of narrative, eschewing emotion yet retaining empathy with the wretched victims of those struggles. Your reviewer found no fact to discount, and few conclusions to dispute.

Summary

Post-Cold War Latin America seems to be following a strong if irregular trajectory to full political and economic modernity. En route, old customs and values from Indo-America, the Iberian Peninsula, and Africa are being modified and sensibly adapted to a careful pursuit of that goal. Latin America may not end up looking like US beltway communities with street signs in Spanish or Portuguese, but it may well do a better job than the Colossus of the North has done in melding the old with the new. The estimate from this corner is that readers of these books, and keen observers of Latin America, will see that neither the Black Legend nor the neo-Marxist worldview ever did have any real connection to this vital region.

BIBLIOGRAPHY

Alvarez, Sonia E., Evelina Dagnino, and Arturo Escobar. *Cultures of Politics, Politics of Cultures: Re-visioning Latin American Social Movements.* Boulder, Colo.: Westview Press, 1998.

Bartell, Ernest, and Leigh A. Payne, eds. *Business and Democracy in Latin America.* Pittsburgh: Univ. of Pittsburgh Press, 1995.

Buckman, Robert T. *Latin America, 1998.* 32d ed.; Harper's Ferry, W. Va.: Stryker-Post, 1998.

Clinton, William J. *A National Security Strategy for a New Century.* Washington: The White House, 1997.

Cockcroft, James D. *Latin America: History, Politics, and U.S. Policy*. 2d ed.; Chicago: Nelson-Hall Publishers, 1997.

Collier, Simon, Thomas E. Skidmore, and Harold Blakemore, eds. *The Cambridge Encyclopedia of Latin America and the Caribbean*. 2d ed.; New York: Cambridge Univ. Press, 1992.

Dominguez, Jorge I., ed. *International Security & Democracy: Latin America and the Caribbean in the Post-War Era*. Pittsburgh: Univ. of Pittsburgh Press, 1998.

Herring, Hubert. *A History of Latin America from the Beginnings to the Present*. 3d ed.; New York: Knopf, 1968.

Keen, Benjamin, ed. *Latin American Civilization: History & Society, 1492 to the Present*. 6th ed.; Boulder, Colo.: Westview Press, 1996.

Loveman, Brian. *The Constitution of Tyranny: Regimes of Exception in Spanish America*. Pittsburgh: Univ. of Pittsburgh Press, 1993.

Mainwaring, Scott, and Timothy R. Scully. *Building Democratic Institutions: Party Systems in Latin America*. Stanford, Calif.: Stanford Univ. Press, 1995.

Mares, David R., ed. *Civil-Military Relations: Building Democracy and Regional Security in Latin America, Southern Asia, and Central Europe*. "Latin America in Global Perspective" series. Boulder, Colo.: Westview Press, 1998.

McClintock, Cynthia. *Revolutionary Movements in Latin America: El Salavador's FMLN and Peru's Shining Path*. Washington: US Institute of Peace Press, 1998.

Ramsey, Russell W. *Guardians of the Other Americas: Essays on the Military Forces of Latin America*. Lanham, Md.: Univ. Press of America, 1997.

_____. "Neo-Marxism Rides the Black Legend," *Journal of Low Intensity Conflict & Law Enforcement*. 6 (Winter 1997), 41-47.

Schulz, Donald E. *The Role of the Armed Forces in the Americas: Civil-Military Relations for the 21st Century*. Carlisle Barracks, Pa.: US Army War College, Strategic Studies Institute, 1998.

Schutte, Ofelia. *Cultural Identity and Social Liberation in Latin American Thought*. Albany, N.Y.: SUNY-Albany, 1993.

Skidmore, Thomas E. "Studying the History of Latin America: A Case of Hemispheric Convergence," *Latin American Research Review*. 33 (Winter 1998).

Weidner, Glenn R. "Overcoming the Power Gap: Reorienting the Inter-American System for Hemispheric Security." Occasional paper, Wetherhead Center for International Affairs. Boston-Harvard Univ., 1998.

Wiarda, Howard J. and Harvey F. Kline, eds. *Latin American Politics and Development*. 4th ed.; Boulder, Colo.: Westview Press, 1996.

The Reviewer: Russell W. Ramsey is a civilian professor at the US Army School of the Americas. He holds the Ph.D. degree in Latin American history from the University of Florida and has written many articles and books on Latin American military topics.

Russell W. Ramsey, Ph.D., D.Min.

Security Cooperation in the Western Hemispheric:
Resolving the Ecuador-Peru Conflict.
<u>Parameters</u> Winter 1999/2000

By Gabriel Marcella and Richard Downes.
Boulder, Colo.: Lynne Rienner, 1999. 256 pp. $45.00. Reviewed by
Russell W. Ramsey, Ph.D., professor of Latin American security
Studies, US Army School of the Americas.

Professors Gabriel Marcella of the US Army War College and Richard
Downes at the University of Miami North-South Center combine efforts here as
editors and partial authors of a classic in the literature of conflict resolution. The
preface by Ambassador Luigi R. Einaudi, US Special Envoy for the Ecuador-
Peru Conflict, 1995-1998, certifies the precision of the diplomatic issues and
traces the excellent military diplomacy described in the book. The introduction,
by Marcella and Downes, is arguably the most complete and objective short
summary yet written on the Ecuador-Peru border dispute.

David Scott Palmer, professor of international relations at Boston University,
surveys the search for conflict resolution in Chapter 1. Under the Rio-Protocol of
1942, following Peru's 1941 armed foray into the disputed zone, the United
States, Argentina, Brazil, and Chile sponsored the overall peace process, but
Ecuador and Peru were named guarantors of the eventual boundary determination
process. Palmer concludes that the Organization of American States (OAS) was
willing to broker a peace, but that Ecuador and Peru felt that the four overall
guarantors named in 1942 could move faster to resolve the crisis. He further
opines that without the military diplomacy achieved under the Military Observer
Mission to Ecuador and Peru (MOMEP), the January-February 1995 crisis might
never have been resolved.

Colonel Glenn R. Weidner, US Army, was US Contingent Commander of
MOMEP, working under General Barry McCaffrey, Commander-in-Chief, US
Southern Command. In Chapter 2, Weidner describes the incredibly complex
command structure, with a Brazilian general as overall coordinator. The four-
point work plan created and carried out seems simple and logical: preparatory
work, supervision of cease-fire, separation of forces, and
demilitarization/demobilization. But as Weidner lays out the competing forces
and actors, the reader comes to see that bringing this plan to fruition was a
miracle in military diplomacy. One example of this was US Southern
Command's insistence on the immediate creation of a demilitarized zone as a
precondition for operations, possibly driven by the Clinton Administration's
Somalian disaster just weeks before. The Brazilian coordinator, Lieutenant
General Candido Vargas de Freire, and MOMEP both thought that a

demilitarized zone should be the sought-for end state, with MOMEP in the meanwhile moving directly to separate forces in the conflict zone.

In Chapter 3, Adrian Bonilla, Deputy Director, Latin American Faculty of Social Studies, Ecuador, evaluates the conflict resolution process from the Ecuadorian viewpoint. His overall conclusion is optimistic. In Chapter 4, Enrique Obando, a Peruvian professor of national security studies, evaluates the conflict resolution process from the Peruvian side. He details the huge military cost to Peru of the conflict, just under $100 million (US), and blames Ecuador for the January 1995 attack.

Patrice Franko teaches economics and international studies at Colby College in Waterville, Maine. Her Chapter 5 presents a strategic survey of military downsizing on the South American continent. She reaches the conclusion that the downward trend in the regional arms race is better served by citizen appeal to each country's legislative body, rather than by arbitrary denials of US security assistance. Eliezer Rizzo de Oliveira is professor of political science at the University of Campinas in Sao Paulo, Brazil. He Chapter 6 surveys Brazilian diplomatic leadership in the 1995 Ecuador-Peru crisis, concluding that it led Brazil and the OAS into stronger roles in conflict prevention.

Edgardo Mercado Jarrin, former Prime Minister, Foreign Minister, War Minister, and army commander in Peru, argues in Chapter 7 that Ecuador was responsible for the "War in the Cenepa." While he considers the post-1995 era the most hopeful for conflict solution negotiations , he warns that Peru can resume an armed posture or even invade Ecuadorian military bases if negotiations fail. David Mares, who teaches political science at the University of California in San Diego, presents in Chapter 8 the results of public opinion polls taken after the 1995 conflict. He concludes that Ecuador must concede more than Peru if the long-standing border conflict is to be solved. Bertha Garcia Gallegos, Director of Interamerican Studies at the Catholic Pontifical University in Quito, Ecuador, repeats in Chapter 9 an old Ecuadorian theme that the 1942 Protocol was unjust to Ecuador and "inexecutable," but she holds out future regional social and economic development as the way to end the "culture of conflict" between both countries.

Finally, Marcella and Downes conclude with an insightful analysis of Latin American military diplomacy in the context of the 1995 MOMEP effort. They bravely venture a long-term solution for the Ecuador-Peru border conflict.

Four conclusions emerge here. First, the total MOMEP process was a diplomatic event of universal importance that would have been, were the major US news media more attuned to strategic analysis and genuine mechanisms for peace, a "top ten" event of 1995. The MOMEP process, with coordinated civilian and military diplomacy, is a paradigm for successful peace operations. Building hemispheric military-to-military contacts pays off in conflict resolution. Second, this book joins an elite body of diplomatic literature with such works as

Manley O. Hudson's *Verdict of the League* (Boston: World Peace Foundation, 1932), an account of the League of Nations peace process in 1932 for the Leticia border conflict between Peru and Colombia. Third, the valiant shuttle diplomacy of Luigi R. Einaudi in this matter places him in a league with Joel R. Poinsett, US Minister to Mexico, in the tumultuous years before the US-Mexican War, and with William Walker, US Ambassador to El Salvador in the early 1990s when the civil war was winding down. Fourth, the military diplomacy both performed and then witnessed in this book by Colonel Glenn R. Weidner places him in an elite group with the stalwart life-saving action of (then) Lieutenant Colonel Douglas MacArthur at Veracruz, Mexico, in 1914; US Navy Captain Edward L. Beach, Sr., at Port-au-Prince, Haiti, in 1915; and General Matthew B. Ridgway at Bogota, Colombia, in April 1948.

This book and its protagonists should be part of any foreign relations discussion in the United States addressing where conflict is likely to occur.

Russell W. Ramsey, Ph.D., D.Min.

Strategic Reading on Latin America
<u>Parameters</u> Spring 2000
RUSSELL W. RAMSEY

As we begin a new century, a bright shining star in Latin American history is an edited work from professors Lewis Hanke and Jane M. Rausch titled *People and Issues in Latin American History: From Independence to the Present* (2d ed., 1998). All the great names and issues both salutary and troubling in the region's history since the early 1800s are here in short, pithy readings, edited with honesty and elegance. Sadly, Professor Hanke, one of Latin American history's grand old men and certainly the premier scholar of the Western Hemisphere's human rights tradition, passed away before this superb volume was published. Here we can read Simon Bolivar's appeal to Bolivians to proclaim a constitution based on principles traced from ancient Greece, and we can find three different appraisals of Fidel Castro's Cuban revolution. Also in the mix are short, pertinent readings on land tenure, *caudillismo*, urban society, industrialization, Latin American views of the North America giant, and much more. For any introductory course on Latin America, this is the perfect book to read in conjunction with Robert T. Buckman's regional introduction, *Latin America 1999*, from the excellent Stryker-Post series.

Thomas O'Brien's 1998 work *The Century of U.S. Capitalism in Latin America* and Terry L. McCoy's *The 1999 Latin American Business Environment: An Assessment* offer the reader a nicely opposed pair of views on the region's current economic situation. For Professor O'Brien, all US investment in Latin America has been a manipulative, profit-seeking venture that has contributed to undemocratic governments and societies. His factual descriptions of US investment and its political consequences are quite good. For Professor McCoy, the regional economic climate is guardedly optimistic, and neo-liberalism is an authentic world trend with overall positive trajectories for Latin America.

Daniel Castro's edited volume *Revolutions and Revolutionaries* (1999) and Kevin J. Middlebrook's edited collection *Electoral Observation and Democratic Transitions in Latin America* (1998) offer comparative strategic insights on the political condition of the region. Castro's revolutionary potpourri shows how the indigenous social and economic injustice issues within Latin America were manipulated by both giants during the Cold War, and have now died back into specific armed challenges heavily connected to the drug war in Colombia and Peru. Middlebrook's work is a good portrait of what election supervision efforts can do with their often limited resources; one is struck by how much more successful these efforts have been in the Western Hemisphere than in the Eastern Hemisphere.

Russell W. Ramsey, Ph.D., D.Min.

Brian Loveman's 1999 volume *For la Patria: Politics and the Armed Forces in Latin America* revisits the tempestuous field of the Latin American military forces and their role in modern politics. He examines their historical status as independent actors functioning in politically and economically nonintegrated societies, concluding that military attitudes now tend to accept democracy but that military coups d'etat could reoccur if economic development fails in the region. Your reviewer examines the history of Latin American military behavior and the US mentorship role in the second printing of the 1997 volume *Guardians of the Other Americas: Essays on the Military Forces of Latin America.* A 1999 follow-up volume, *Addenda to Guardians of the Other Americas*, offers several recently published essays examining policy and behavioral aspects of the Latin American armed forces. These essays will be incorporated into the next edition of the original work, which is currently under publication in Spanish in Quito, Ecuador, by the Defense Ministry.

Stephen C. Rabe's 1999 work *The Most Dangerous Area in the World: John F. Kennedy Confronts Communist Revolution in Latin America* continues his 1988 critique of the Eisenhower-era anticommunism policy in Latin America. In the present work, he pounds on the Kennedy counterinsurgency doctrine as basically unnecessary and productive of abusive, retrograde regimes, in total contravention of the noble ideals presented in the Alliance for Progress. Professor Rabe's historical trace of the Kennedy-era counterinsurgency doctrine is excellent; your reviewer can attest to this as a first-person participant as well as a historian of the issue. The harsh historical judgment seems unwarranted, however, given the fact that the end product of the counterinsurgency policy in 1990 was a region ready for and generally accepting of democratization and economic liberalization, and given that the internal defense of small societies during great-power struggles is never pretty to watch. One can conclude that without the counterinsurgency policy started by President Kennedy and continued by every President thereafter, Latin America would have suffered a half dozen communist regimes, and the "basket-case country in the back yard" population would be much larger than merely Cuba and Haiti. Richard D. Downie's 1998 *Learning from Conflict: The U.S. Military in Vietnam, El Salvador, and the Drug War* is the best operational description yet written on the US counterinsurgency policy. However, his quest for the correct universal application that would have worked well in El Salvador and in the Colombian drug war is perhaps quixotic.

We shift now to individual country situations. Richard C. Thornton's 1998 book *The Falklands Sting: Reagan, Thatcher, and Argentina's Bomb* is a real James Bond story at the national security policy level. He examines the idea that not only did Prime Minister Margaret Thatcher invent her "splendid little war" in 1981 to shore up sagging Conservative policies, but also that President Ronald Reagan's national security team actually supported Dame Margaret's war as a way of defusing the production of nuclear weapons in the Southern Cone of South America. The review of diplomatic events is solid history; one can accept or reject Thornton's Byzantine explorations.

Lee K. Durham's occasional paper "Reality v. Perception: Democracy Under President Fujimori" (1999) is one of the few pieces extant that examines what Latin American military professionals and their families actually think about incomplete democracies such as Peru under President Alberto Fujimori. Professors Gabriel Marcella and Richard Downes edited *Security Cooperation in the Western Hemisphere: Resolving the Ecuador-Peru Conflict* (1999). It shows how US Ambassador Luigi Einaudi and US Army Colonel Glenn R. Weidner led peacemaking efforts that resolved the 1995 border conflict between Ecuador and Peru in a manner that should become a world model for conflict resolution (for a full review, see the Winter 1999-2000 issue of *Parameters*, pp. 137-39.

Professor Harvey F. Kline's 1999 study *State Building and Conflict Resolution in Colombia, 1986-1994* deals with the troubling question of why a country so excellent in rural peacemaking in the 1960s could have fallen victim to the FARC narco-guerrillas in the 1990s. He traces the ways in which Presidents Virgilio Barco (1986-1990) and Cesar Gaviria (1990-1994) failed to build a unified civil-military peacemaking system in the rural zones long flagellated by the earlier banditry and guerrilla violence. Canadian Professor Dennis Rempe has recently produced two important articles on Colombia, en route to a full-length treatment on rural violence in Colombia since the 1970s. "The Origin of Internal Security in Colombia" will appear in the Winter 1999 issue of *Small Wars & Insurgencies*, and "An American Trojan Horse? Eisenhower, Latin America, and the Development of U.S. Internal Security Policy, 1954-60" appeared in the Spring 1999 issue. Rempe's work will ultimately be phase two of your reviewer's forthcoming *Soldados y guerrilleros*, the history of the Colombian violence from 1946 to 1965.

Thomas L. Percy's 1999 work *We Answer Only to God: Politics and the Military in Panama, 1903-1947* provides a vital and completely original theory of civil-military relations in Latin America. Percy opines that the US policy of demilitarizing Panama by means of institutionalizing a national police resulted in a highly politicized police institution which, in fact, made and broke governments in Panama during the years when textbooks tended to label Panama a democracy.

The quality of scholarly books about Latin America which examine national security issues is much higher than it was during the Cold War. Little by little, the scholarly world is abandoning the lamentable predisposition to see the region through the eyes of neo-Marxism and dwell more on the actual political and economic setting, with sincere analysis of US regional policy. All of this bodes well for the US policy of military-to-military engagement. Despite vicious accusations from bitter neo-Marxists who cannot admit that Latin America rejected their millenarian dream, the US Army's tutorial role in Latin America since 1940, when it took on that role, is an achievement that redounds heavily to the institution's credit.

The Reviewer: Russell W. Ramsey is a civilian professor at the US Army School of The Americas. He holds the Ph.D. degree in Latin American history from the University of Florida and has written many articles and books on Latin American military topics.

BIBLIOGRAPHY

Buckman, Robert T. *Latin America 1999.* 33d ed. Harpers Ferry, W. Va.: Stryker-Post Publications, 1999.

Castro, Daniel, ed. *Revolutions and revolutionaries.* Jaguar Books Series. Wilmington, Del.: Scholarly Resources, 1999.

Downie, Richard D. *Learning from Conflict: The U.S. Military in Vietnam, El Salvador, and the Drug War.* Westport, Conn.: Praeger, 1998.

Durham, Lee K. "Reality v. Perception: Democracy Under President Fujimori." Occasional paper, Troy State University, Ft. Benning, Ga., 1999.

Hanke, Lewis, and Jane M. Rausch, eds. *People and Issues in Latin American History from Independence to the Present.* 2d ed. Princeton, N.J.: Marcus Wiener Publishers, 1998.

Kline, Harvey F. *State Building and Conflict Resolution in Colombia, 1986-1994.* Tuscaloosa: Univ. of Alabama Press, 1999.

Loveman, Brian. *For la Patria: Politics and the Armed Forces in Latin America.* Jaguar Books Series. Wilmington, Del.: Scholarly Resources, 1999.

Marcella, Gabriel, and Richard Downes, eds. *Security Cooperation in the Western Hemisphere: Resolving the Ecuador-Peru Conflict.* Coral Gables, Fla.: North-South Center Press, Univ. of Miami, 1999.

McCoy, Terry L. *The 1999 Latin American Business Environment: An Assessment.* Center for International Business Education and Research. Gainesville: Univ. of Florida Press, 1999.

Middlebrook, Kevin J., ed. *Electoral Observation and Democratic Transitions in Latin America.* San Diego: Univ. of California, San Diego, 1998.

O'Brien, Thomas. *The Century of U.S. Capitalism in Latin America.* Albuquerque: Univ. of New Mexico Press, 1998.

Pearcy, Thomas L. *We Answer Only to God: Politics and the Military in Panama, 1903-1947.* Albuquerque: Univ. of New Mexico Press, 1999.

Rabe, Stephen C. *The Most Dangerous Area in the World: John F. Kennedy Confronts Communist Revolution in Latin America.* Chapel Hill: Univ. of North Carolina Press, 1999.

Ramsey, Russell W., ed. *Addenda to Guardians of the Other Americas: Essays on the Military Forces of Latin America.* Columbus, Ga.: VIP Publishing, 1999.

_____, ed. *Guardians of the Other Americas: Essays on the Military Forces of Latin America.* Lanham, Md.: Univ. Press of America, 1997.

_____, ed. *Soldados y guerrilleros.* Bogotz: Presna Tercer Mundo, forthcoming.

Rempe, Dennis. "The Origin of Internal Security in Colombia." *Small Wars & Insurgencies*, 10 (Winter 1999).

_____. "An American Trojan Horse? Eisenhower, Latin America, and the Development of U.S. Internal Security Policy, 1954-60." *Small Wars & Insurgencies*, 10 (Spring 1999), 34-64.

Thornton, Richard C. *The Falklands Sting: Reagan, Thatcher, and Argentina's Bomb.* Washington: Brassey's, 1998.

Russell W. Ramsey, Ph.D., D.Min.

Strategic Reading on Latin America
Parameters Winter 2000/2001
RUSSELL W. RAMSEY

The quality of strategic literature in the English language on Latin American security issues continued to improve. While the success of democratization and privatization in Latin America is the subject of wholesome debate, there can be little doubt that better books on regional security issues now exist for productive use by the military analyst, policymaker, professor, or entrepreneur than could be found during the Cold War.

Once again, Robert Buckman's annual entry from the Stryker-Post Series, *Latin America, 2000*, wins the prize as the one-volume book on choice for the strategic analyst. This is the 35th edition on the Latin American region, updated annually by the professor of journalism from the University of Louisiana at Lafayette. Buckman is also an Army Reservist with a Joint Chiefs of Staff billet. His thumbnail regional introduction is guardedly optimistic; his country-by-country presentations give historical sketches followed by recent economic, political, and national security trends. Editor Phil Stryker has made this series remarkable for ideological neutrality, factual integrity, and low cost; Buckman's summary on the Colombian drug war is excellent.

The next book in order of value is Patrice Franko's unique volume, *The Puzzle of Latin American Economic Development*. Franko has translated the jungle of economic terminology about Latin America, often distorted by the writer's own ideological slant, into clear, objective words, showing the humanistic dimension of the various policies. Thus, Raul Prebisch's import substitution and ultra-nationalistic economic policies are explained as an unsuccessful alternative to economic liberalism in the late 1950s. Professor Franko connects these policies to the dependency theory of Fernando Henrique Cardoso and others, showing how this interpretation led to unsuccessful experiments with Marxist economics in the Western Hemisphere. After detailing the paradigm shift to the neo-liberalism of the 1980s, she revisits her five-point agenda for modernization stated at the outset of the book. These issues are: balance between internal and external economic activity, promoting stability alongside change in economic policy, balancing the needs of the poor with those of the entrepreneurial sector, the role of the state in development, and the conflict between contemporary economic success and future strength. For any course or seminar on the economics of regional security in the Western Hemisphere, this is the book of choice.

Professors Michael LaRosa and Frank O.Mora have jointly written and edited *Neighborly Adversaries: Readings in U.S.-Latin American Relations*. It includes a survey essay by LaRosa and Mora, followed by six sections of readings on US-Latin American relations, each with a summary essay by the editors. The six sections include a philosophical overview, the 19th century, the 20th century to World War II, the early revolutions following World War II, the regional conflict era when the Cold War spilled over into Latin America, and the post-Cold War period. By carefully culling the best and most typical portrayals of US-Latin American relations in each of these eras, the authors bring sunlight and logic to much that has been dark and polemical within the scholarly community. They quote Ambassador George Kennan's 1950 analysis of communism in Latin America, attempting to tie the region to his earlier Cold War paradigm known as the "Mr. X" article, that great 1947 policy watershed which initiated the era of deterrence and containment. They extract the core of President John F. Kennedy's rationale for the Alliance for Progress, and also a salient critique on why the alliance did not create political democracies capable of withstanding the impetus to military dictatorship during the Cold War assault on several governments by Soviet-sponsored Cuban subversion. This excellent book gives the reader a way to view US relations with Latin America without diving into the murky waters of ideology; Professors LaRosa and Mora show the strengths and the weaknesses of the US national security policies, the region's governments, and the several kinds of revolutionaries who challenged the existence of some governments. Again, this is the clear choice for a single-volume reader on US-Latin American relations.

John Peeler's 1998 volume *Building Democracy in Latin America* examines the elusive question that scholars and policymakers alike have examined so often, namely, the fact that Latin America has historically tried to portray itself as a region of peace-loving democratic republics but has produced several brutal dictatorships and a larger number of partial democracies. He establishes his position early that democracy in Latin America is possible but not inevitable. In the introductory chapter he examines the political theory extant in the establishing of Latin America's nation-states, concluding that shortcomings of implementation are the cause of Latin America's departure from the theoretical models of democracy. Professor Peeler's subsequent chapter on early Latin American democracies concludes that variegated evolution from a "civil oligarchy" into a full democracy occurred in Costa Rica, Colombia, Chile, and Venezuela. Choosing Paraguay, Mexico, and Cuba for his chapter on authoritarian regimes, the author suggests that none of these three countries rests upon an inevitable trajectory toward full democracy, yet that each has provided some important democratic features. In his overall evaluation he equates democratic success with strong linkage between electoral choice and public policy, concluding that Latin America's history of balancing radical reform with governmental stability under a constitution will provide some successful governing systems. But Peeler finds neither populism nor neo-liberalism to be acceptable panaceas, returning again to the paradigm of a successful linkage between voter will and public policy. This book is not comprehensive, save for its superb bibliography, but it does offer vital new ways to evaluate emerging democracy in post-Cold War Latin America.

A longer book of edited readings with commentary is Larry Diamond, et al., *Democracy in Developing Countries: Latin America*. For Central America the authors address Mexico and Costa Rica; the Dominican Republic is the Caribbean entry; and the South American continent is represented by essays on Argentina, Brazil, Chile, Colombia, Peru, and Venezuela. Although not written to a precise format, each essay includes historical trends, recent economic development, recent political evolution, and evaluation of overall political-economic integration. Some include a discrete section on US policy toward the subject country, and some include a prognosis for future democratic performance. The introduction is, in essence, an essay on what constitutes a democracy in Latin America. It follows the methodology and contents seen in Professor Seymour Martin Lipset's 1981 classic *Political Man: The Social Bases of Politics*. (While Lipset, the nation's professor emeritus of socio-political integration, is one of the editors of this collection, none of the essays appears under his by-line.) The introduction and nine country analyses are strong, but the book fails in not having a final essay that synthesizes the trends. Each essay, nevertheless, is a stand alone gem, written by an acknowledged national expert. The book would serve well for a course on comparative politics in Latin America, and as background reading for national security professionals who will work in the countries analyzed.

Joseph S. Tulchin and Ralph H. Espach are coauthors and coeditors of *Security Cooperation in the Caribbean Basin*. This region is the maritime front door of the United Sates, over whose stability and control a century ago the United States became a world-ranked naval power. Following the authors' joint introductory essay about the region's strategic importance, there are three topical sections: the post-Cold War Caribbean security agenda, nontraditional threats to that region, and cooperative security measures extant or planned. "Drugs and the Emerging Security Agenda in the Caribbean," by Professor Ivelaw L. Griffith, is one of the finest essays available on the topic. Item by item, Professor Griffith names a condition pertaining to the illicit drug problem, derives the security threat it imposes, and then connects it to Caribbean and US society. At essay's end, the reader can see how comprehensive and overwhelming the illegal narcotics plague really is, yet can also see the sectoral linkage behind both the threat and the possible solutions. "A Call for the Redefinition of Regional and National interests," is a short essay by Dominican Republic General Jose E. Noble Espejo. He points out that most security measures in the Caribbean have traditionally been taken bilaterally between the United States and each of the small countries, and calls for the adoption of a truly regional anti-narcotics strategy. The summary essay by Tulchin and Espach posits that the Caribbean Economic Community (CARICOM) and a Caribbean anti-narcotics strategy cannot succeed independently, and that each must be coordinated politically with the other. They also opine that the United States' "anachronistic stalemate with Cuba" is counterproductive to overall regional security. This book should be mandatory reading for any college course on the Caribbean region and is a model for short, excellent texts in regional security studies.

MERCOSUR: Regional Integration, World Markets is a 1999 study authored and edited by Professor Riordan Roett. MERCOSUR is the world's only regional trade agreement under the World Trade Organization concept which uses a Spanish acronym—for Mercado Comun Sureño (in English, "Southern Common Market") based on its primary members Argentina, Brazil, and Chile, with Paraguay and Uruguay in an affiliated status. The issue is vital to Western Hemisphere security, for the so-called "ABC" countries (Argentina, Brazil, and Chile) anchor the South American continent, and upon them depends the region's stability and future growth. Following an introduction by Roett, there are essays by experts on trade. Brazil, industrialization, membership, and relationships with the European Economic Union. The chapter on Brazil is critical to any study of regional security, for the South American giant conducts 70 percent of all MERCOSUR's trade and is the world's 9th-ranked economic power. In his summary essay, Roett shows how partisan squabbling and petty nationalistic posturing in the United States damages MERCOSUR as well as US interests in that potentially powerful region. This book provides invaluable readings for a course on Latin American economics, as well as for studying regional security.

While other excellent English-language books exist, this collection will take the serious student to Latin American security issues deeply enough into the milieu to formulate solid policy ideas.

BIBLIOGRAPHY

Buckman, Robert T. *Latin America, 2000.* 35th ed. Harpers Ferry, W. Va.: Stryker-Post, 2000.

Diamond, Larry, Jonathan Hartlyn, Juan I. Linz, and Seymour Martin Lipset, eds. *Democracy in Developing Countries: Latin America.* 2d ed. Boulder, Colo.: Lynne Rienner, 1999.

Franko, Patrice. *The Puzzle of Latin American Economic Development.* Lanham, Md.: Rowman & Littlefield, 1999.

Henderson, James D., Helen Delpar, and Maurice P. Brungardt. *A Reference Guide to Latin American History.* Armonk, N.Y.: M. E. Sharpe, 1000.

LaRosa, Michael, and Frank O. Mora, eds. *Neighborly Adversaries: Readings in U.S.-Latin American Relations.* Lanham, Md.: Rowman & Littlefield, 1999.

Peeler, John. *Building Democracy in Latin America.* Boulder, Colo.: Lynne Rienner, 1998.

Roett, Riordan, ed. *MERCOSUR: Regional Integration, World Markets.* Boulder, Colo.: Lynne Rienner, 1999.

Tulchin, Joseph S., and Ralph H. Espach. *Security Cooperation in the Caribbean Basin.* Boulder, Colo.: Lynne Rienner, 2000.

The Reviewer: Dr. Russell W. Ramsey, Ph.D., D. Min., was Professor of Latin American Security Affairs, US Army School of the Americas (USARSA) from June 1992 through August 2000. In September, he retired from the Civil Service and returned to the School of the Americas as Visiting Professor of Latin American Security Affairs from Troy State University, a role in which he will assist in the transition from USARSA to the new congressionally authorized configuration.

Russell W. Ramsey, Ph.D., D.Min.

Hispanic American Historical Review

Duke University Press

The Bolivian Diary of Ernesto Che Guevara. Edited by MARY-ALICE WATERS. New York: Pathfinder Press, 1994. Photographs. Maps. Notes. Glossary. Index. 467 pp. Cloth, $55.00. Paper, $21.95.

Episodes of the Cuban Revolutionary War, 1956-58. Edited by MARY-ALICE WATERS. New York: Pathfinder Press, 1996. Photographs. Notes. Glossary. Index. X, 483 pp. Cloth, $65.00. Paper, $23.95.

A team of Cuban scholars has worked for a decade on an edited set of Ernesto "Che" Guevara's memoirs on the Cuban Revolutionary War, published as *Pasajes de la Guerra revolucionaria* (Havana: Editorial Politica, 1996). Mary-Alice Waters, a writer and longtime champion of the Cuban Revolution, worked simultaneously to prepare an English version, the *Episodes of the Cuban Revolutionary War, 1956-58*. Waters and the Cuban editing team started earlier on the other Che Guevara memoirs, the less complete account of his fatal expedition in Bolivia. These essays emerged as *El diario del Che en Bolivia* (Havana: Editora Politica, 1987, 1988); they were refined and translated into English as *The Bolivian Diary*.

Che Guevara belongs to an exclusive fraternity of revolutionary theoreticians who were also force commanders in the field. His first literary effort, *La Guerra de guerrillas*, was really a long essay, part theory and part application. A quick translation by the Central Intelligence Agency went to the desk of Robert F. Kennedy, soon to be attorney general and Cold War adviser extraordinaire to President-elect John F. Kennedy. The Kennedy brothers, hoping to build support for the forthcoming Alliance for Progress, perceived Guevara's piece as the expression of a serious threat to their hemispheric view. Consequently, a month before JFK's inauguration, orders were given to the U.S. Army to begin training the Latin American armies and security forces in counterinsurgency and nation-building programs.

In the early 1960s, English translations of Che Guevara's "On Guerrilla Warfare" came out in *Evergreen, Ramparts*, and *Monthly Review*: other Guevara essays followed. Gathered mostly from Cuba's *Verde Olivo* magazine, they were translated into English by Victoria Ortiz and published as *Reminiscences of the Cuban Revolutionary War* (1968). The same year, John Gerassi edited Guevara's essays and published them as *Venceremos! The Speeches and Writings of Ernesto Che Guevara* (1968). The Gerassi volume contains the essays on the battles against the Fulgencio Batista government, Guevara's political and economic theories, and the original "On Guerrilla Warfare."

The present work edited by Waters, *Episodes*, corrects hundreds of little errors that have crept into the Che Guevara essays; it also fully identifies figures alluded to or previously identified only by *noms de guerre*. Photographs, a glossary of terms, an order-of-battle chart, and rosters of names with minibiographies make this work mandatory reading for students of the Cuban Revolution.

Che Guevara organized a team of Cuban internationalists volunteers to fight alongside followers of Patrice Lumumba in Zaire, then called the Congo. Guevara's work and message were a major force at the January 1966 Tricontinental Conference in Havana. In November of that year, he joined the guerrilla cadre had had inserted into the Bolivian altiplano, and he kept a diary during the ten-month effort to implant a revolution. Betrayed in the field, captured, and executed in October 1967 by the Bolivian administration of Rene Barrientos, he was immediately enshrined in the Valhalla of fallen revolutionaries. Aleida March obtained the diary—actually in two separate segments—and arranged for its publication under Cuban government auspices.

Daniel James translated and edited Guevara's field memoirs as *The Complete Bolivian Diaries of Che Guevara and Other Captured Documents* (1968). Until now the James volume has stood as the definitive Guevara memoir on the Bolivia episodes, just as the Ortiz and Gerassi volumes have been the sources for Guevara's revolutionary theories and his field command role in Cuba. Recently, however, Bolivian government officials have cooperated with Cuban authorities to release and validate more documents. Michael Taber and Michael Baumann worked with Waters to render the present version, *The Bolivian Diary*. Newly translated, it contains field notes by Inti Peredo and other field commanders who corroborate Guevara's notes and also fill in gaps.

Waters' meticulously edited pair of volumes is now the best original source for English-speaking scholars. Her attention to detail and her precision do not overcome the rough eloquence that was Guevara's style; the transcendental message of a new moral order bites through the prose with deceptive simplicity.

The Uruguayan post José Rodó created, in the early 1900s, a Latin American metaphorical persona called Ariel, a romantic yet legitimate Icarus whose wings always melted in the heat of competition with the North American giant. Ernesto "Che" Guevara became Latin America's Ariel incarnate during the Cold War. He blended Marxist political and economic constructs of another time and culture with the essential spirituality of Latin America. Waters' meticulous volumes do for Guevara's work and writing what Arrian of Cappadocia did for Alexander the Great: preserve the thought and work of a tempestuous, controversial figure with honesty and artistic grace.

RUSSELL W. RAMSEY, U.S. Army School of the Americas.

Russell W. Ramsey, Ph.D., D.Min.

Hispanic American Historical Review

August 1999

We Answer Only to God: Politics and the Military in Panama, 1903-1947.
By THOMAS L. PEARCY. Albuquerque: University of New Mexico Press,
1998. Maps. Tables. Figures. Appendixes. Notes. Bibliography. Index. Xvi,
231 pp. Cloth, $45.00.

Much of Latin American history portrays Panamanian national life as a by-
product of Spanish, Colombian, French, and United States hegemonic policy. In
the early 1980s, geographic determinism—the isthmus as a convenient
commercial terminus, or as a site for a good dig—gave way to Panamanian
nationalism as the focal theme. By the late 1980s, revisionism had moved
onward to focus upon militarized isthmian politics, culminating in Operation Just
Cause in 1989.

In *We Answer Only to God*, Thomas L. Pearcy connects, as he states, "the
social history literature with the institutional literature," thus seeking "to situate
the military more fully within the broader context of a sovereign, independent
republic." Between 1960 and 1962, this reviewer was a United States Army
officer in the old Panama Canal Zone, and was privileged to hear the young
captain Omar Torrijos and other officers of the Panamanian Guardia Nacional
articulate their dreams for an authentic nation-state. Pearcy here shines his
interpretive light on subsequent events that might be called a politics of police
praetorianism, but he also derives a theory showing that Panamanian police
praetorianism from 1967 to 1989 had authentic roots that dated from earlier
times.

The section on colonial history is a survey. In it the author argues that
incipient Panamanian nationalism was thwarted by Spanish colonial policy. This
trend, he states, continued when Colombian efforts to create a constitutional
republic with a capital at Bogotá translated into military control over
independence-minded Panamanians. This section also evaluates United States
security measures in Colombia Panama that were instituted between the Bidlack-
Mallarino Treaty of 1846 and the 1903 treaty that produced both rights to the
canal and the U.S.-friendly client-state known as the Republic of Panama.

Pearcy then shows that after 1903, the efforts by United States leaders to
create a legitimate police institution constituted an alternative to the Caribbean
and Central American revolving-door *golpismo* so prevalent in that era. The
stage is set for an original thesis, the emergence of the police institution as the
legitimate vehicle for Panamanian nationalism between 1931 and the advent of
World War II security measures from 1940 to 1942.

Police commanders José Remon and Bolivar Vallarino were thus part of an established political and economic vehicle in the post-World War II era, praetorians who made and unmade politicians. But they were also guardians of a Panamanian nationalism that did not fit the United States regional paradigm for Panama as a tranquil place from which to operate a central and vital waterway. As Pearcy suggests, Omar Torrijos's rising star came from this tradition and was in no way idiosyncratic.

The historian who would evaluate Manuel Noriega as a powerful, nationalist, corrupt megalomaniac, or as a Cold War opportunist, can employ Pearcy's revisionist paradigm to good stead. Pearcy's linking of isthmian social forces in the 1930s to the police institution as spear carrier for authentic Panamanian nationalism between 1967 and 1989 is a splendid and welcome contribution to Latin American history. This book is a model for the analysis of civil-military relations within developing nations in general, and within client-state nations in particular.

RUSSEL W. RAMSEY, United States Army School of the Americas.

Journal of Comparative Strategy
15:109-119, 1996

Hopeful Neolilberals, Derailed Collectivists—Emerging Paradigms on Latin America.

Review by Russell W. Ramsey
Distinguished Resident Professor
U.S. Army School of the Americas
Fort Benning, Georgia, USA

The cold war is over, but Latin America was caught up in its margins from 1947 through 1990. The analytical literature on the region was occasionally good, but always denigrated by the author's need to become positioned on the U.S. political spectrum. To be published on the "other Americas," especially if U.S. policy touched the issue in question, one was either a conservative backing containment or was a leftist and pro-liberationist.

The joke is that the U.S. liberal-conservative political spectrum seldom applied to anything going on in Latin America, but liberals and conservatives went right on "fixing" the region according to their partisan views. It was stability over change, and arms for the military, please, if you were conservative; and it was humanitarian cash plus sometimes even guns for leftist rebels if you were progressive [1].

Hope for a New Literature

In 1995, economic privatization and political democratization are the trendy topics for those who want to publish something about Latin America. From the Rio Conference of 1947 to the stunning upset electoral victory of the Nicaraguan National Opposition Union coalition in 1990, cold war rhetoric reigned at the masthead. United States conservatives found communists lurking behind most social unrest in the region before 1961, while liberals made the case for U.S. sponsorship of progressive Latin American leadership. After 1961, U.S. conservatives warned of Castro-sponsored subversions, while liberals and a vocal leftist component within academia denied the Soviet-Castro threat and openly advocated for progressive and socialist regimes in the region. With little or no ideological help, thank you, from Uncle Sam's partisan warriors on Latin American policy, Latin America produced an authentic regional movement of its own in the late 1970s, looking at modernization models on the rim of Asia, in Eastern Europe, and certainly not discarding the inclusive model of its sometimes clumsy neighbor to the north.

Since 1990, new voices have taken up the interpretive role on Latin America and U.S. policy in that region. One view holds that Latin America is democratizing and privatizing, with some degree of success. The other view is that socialism lost as a result of U.S. National security programs that derailed popular democracy and that today's apparent waves of democratization and privatization are skin-deep, thereby imposing merely temporary delays in the ultimate march to progressivism. These two camps may be called the hopeful neoliberals and the derailed collectivists. The hopeful neoliberals include new types of analysts in their arsenal: the professor of business administration and the bank officer who comprehends the social impact of finance. The derailed collectivists are a disparate mixture. Some are neo-Marxists who still hope to vindicate Cuba's Fidel Castro, Chile's Salvador Allende, El Salvador's "Faribundo Marti" de Liberación Nacional guerrillas, and the Nicaraguan Sandinistas. Others are historians, social scientists, economists, and journalists who admit that neo-Marxism and the Castro model have failed, but who point out that classical liberalism and statist liberalism have also failed in several Latin American countries.

Grappling for the Center of Mass

Robert A. Packenham critiqued the leftist tendencies of U.S. scholars who specialize in Latin America in his study called *The Dependency Movement: Scholarship and Politics in Development Studies* (1992) [2]. Cristobal Kay counterattacked with a withering review of Packenham's book in the British *Journal of Latin American Studies* (May 1994) [3], thereby highlighting the new paradigm. In anticipation of the December 1994 Summit of the Americas in Miami, the U.S. Information Agency and the North-South Center of the University of Miami sponsored an intellectual mountaintop. Voices of privatization and free trade, liberation theology, constitutional democracy, separatist movements, and of collectivist government all were heard and samples of the results were published in Robert S. Leiken's edited volume, *A New Moment in the Americas* [4]. While the essays resonate to the concept of a new moment of opportunity, there was at most a very guarded optimism.

Current History [5] shows the wavering nature of the new paradigm in its annual numbers on Latin America. In 1993, editor William W. Finan was so impressed with Mexico's economic surge that the February issue was devoted entirely to analysis of Uncle Sam's newly prosperous neighbor to the south, and the impact of NAFTA. The March 1993 issue covered the rest of Latin America and again there was visible optimism. By March 1994 a few bubbles had burst, and Finan devoted only the March number of all of Latin America; several of the articles were sourly pessimistic. In February 1995 Finan devoted an issue to Latin America minus Mexico, and to the certain displeasure of such protectionists as Ross Perot, the March issue to North America, which he defined as Mexico, the United States, and Canada, or the North American Free Trade Agreement (NAFTA) basin. Much of this geographically restructured coverage, however, carried a dire tone.

Pierre Etinenne Dostert of the Stryker-Post "World Today" Series has written the Latin America annual volume for many years. His 1995 entry (twenty-first in the series) on the region [6] hides from none of the problems: inflation, debt, corruption, "narcotrafficking," soaring birth rate, and all the rest. Yet he retains the essential optimism about the humane nature of the region that he saw during the cold war years, and he sees new opportunities offered by privatization and democratization.

The Neo-Liberal Optimists

The optimism scenario is primarily an economic paradigm. Latin American governmental leaders in the 1970s perceived that several European and Asian rim nations were doing better with privatization than with the bureaucratically inefficient statist enterprises being operated in Latin American countries then under the economic influence of Argentine economist Raul Prebisch. Selling off nonproductive corporations with bloated personnel rosters carries a price, namely, mass unemployment among a sector possessing the skills to organize revolutions in a hurry if their needs are not met. New investment must be rapidly attracted to provide this new employment. The democratization process is attractive to potential investors, but increased citizen participation in politics occurs just when the most intensely focused popular demand is for employment. Thus there is a potential for a new spiral of government-subsidized employment, thereby tipping the scales back to statist economic policies.

The optimists find mutually supporting dynamics between privatization and democratic pluralization, and they believe that the armed forces will remain constitutionally obedient to civilian authority. Eliana Cardosa and Ann Helwege have authored the most complete descriptive volume, called *Latin America's Economy* (1995) [7]. Strongest are the structural descriptions; analysis of what privatization offers to the masses in a positive sense is limited. Paul W. Drake edited a volume called *Money Doctors, Foreign Debts, and Economic Reforms in Latin American from the 1890s to the Present in 1994* [8]. These essays explain why it is that free market economics have failed before in Latin America. William C. Smith, Carlos H. Acuna, and Eduardo Gamarra cover the economic waterfront topically in their excellent 1994 volume *Latin American Political Economy* in an Age of Neoliberal Reform [9]. These writers do not affirm the impossibility of more failures, but they show convincingly that Latin America has drastically altered the way that it thinks and functions, thereby creating an optimistic tone.

Editor Jaime Suchlicki of *North-South, the Magazine of the Americas* [10] devoted many articles and two special issues to economic privatization. The October-November 1993 issue examined economics in the cone of South America, the basin known by the Spanish acronym for Southern Common Market (MERCOSUR). Articles on the pros and cons of NAFTA appeared with regularity for 3 years. *North-South* devoted the entire November-December 1994 issue to the Summit of the Americas, held at Miami during that time. Lamentably, this was the swan song of a fine magazine.

And Now the Pessimists

Those who are pessimistic about Latin America's future base their position on two things: frustration that the neo-Marxist worldview did not prove itself in the region and an abiding belief that the armed forces of Latin America are hopelessly and permanently predatory. Dispensing with the neo-Marxist worldview is the simple task, despite the existence of two or three dim bulb books alleging to prove that the militant left is alive, well, and highly authentic.

Michale Radu and Vladimir Tismaneanu are Romanian professors working in the United States. Their meticulously researched volume *Latin American Revolutionaries: Groups, Goals, and Methods* (1990) [11] showed neo-Marxism, spearheaded by Fidel Castro after 1967, and traditional Marxism before Castro, to be at most a skin deep European import. Timothy P. Wickham-Crowley analyzed carefully in 1992 the several guerrilla wars in Latin America during the cold war. His results, published as *Guerrillas and Revolution in Latin America: A Comparative Study of Insurgents and Regimes since 1956* [12], showed convincingly that only in Cuba, in 1959 and Nicaragua in 1977 did leftist guerrilla movements within Latin America have anything even close to the requisite popular support for success. In these two cases, Wickham-Crowley found that the margin for supporting Castro in Cuba and the Sandinistas in Nicaragua was not the revolutionary movement itself, but the self-defeating U.S. policy of propping up Mañoso-type regimes (Fulgencio Batista in Cuba and the Somoza dynasty in Nicarague) in the name of preventing communist revolution.

There is more, however, to the pessimism paradigm than sour faces by the academic left over the failure of their heroes to carry out revolutions. Frederick M. Nunn's 1992 study *The Time of the Generals: Latin American Professional Militarism in World Perspective* [13] hypothesized that militarism on the South American continent was linked strongly to a cold war-era French concept of national security, namely, that the armed forces are empowered to identify and neutralize enemies of the state. David Pion-Berlin critiqued this and several other recent books on Latin America's armed forces in his essay "The Armed Forces in Politics: Gains and Snares in Recent Scholarship," *Latin American Research Review* (Spring 1995) [14] by lauding the analysis of Latin American military philosophy, but deploring the unsubstantiated assumption that military hostility for democracy is absolute and permanent. After all, the Latin Americans have historically spent less than 2% of their gross national product on military things, and they have produced only three regional wars. With typically two or less soldiers per 1,000 citizens save in Castro's Cuba, Latin America also has been the world's least militarized region for decades.

William Perry and Max Primorac offered an agenda of legitimate roles for the armed forces of Latin America in "The Inter-American Security Agenda," *Journal of Inter-American Studies and World Affairs* (Spring 1994) [15]. This reviewer showed ways that the armed forces could undergird the economic privatization movement in his article, "The Role of the Latin American Armed Forces in the 1990s," *Strategic Review* (November-December 1992) [16]. Yet Brian Loveman opined that virtually all of Latin America's armed forces would flout both civilian authority and human rights under probable future conditions in his meticulous article "Protected Democracies' and Military Guardianship: Political Transitions in Latin America, 1978-1993," *Journal of Inter-American Studies and World Affairs* (Spring 1994) [17]. Lars Schoultz, William C. Smith, and Augusto Varas authored and edited *Security, Democracy, and Development in U.S.-Latin American Relations* (1994) [18]. While the Latin American contributions describe several new paradigms for regional security forces, most of the U.S. contributors found regional security systems, and the U.S. contribution to those systems, to be of marginal or even negative value.

Whither Foreign Policy?

Abraham F. Lowenthal and Gregory F. Treverton have the best book to date on regional policy. Their 1994 *Latin America in a New World* [19] outlines a hemispheric diplomatic structure keyed logically to the sustainment of privatization and democratization. Robert A. Pastor's 1992 book *Whirlpool: U.S. Foreign Policy Toward Latin America and the Caribbean* [20] is full of good ideas about foreign policy and case studies about useful U.S. assistance to the democratization process. Martha L. Cottam's 1994 study called *Images and Intervention: U.S. Policies in Latin America* [21] is more a reflection of the author's disagreement with past U.S. policy in the Western Hemisphere than a meaningful inventory of workable policies for the present.

I. Erik Kjonnerod edited *Evolving U.S. Strategy for Latin America and the Caribbean* in 1992 [22]. His essays offer explicit ways in which U.S. strategy can undergird economic privatizationand democratic pluralization by presenting courses in military and police professionalism, maintaining cordial military-to-military relationships in the region, and enhancing political and economic dialogue on security issues. This reviewer offered a 10-point menu to this end in "U.S. Strategy for Latin America" appearing in the Autumn 1994 issue of *Parameters* [23].

Is Anybody Right?

For too long, North American writers have regarded Latin America as a backwater in need of having their own correct U.S. views imposed on it. From 1947 to 1990 this exercise in cultural imperialism was organized along the liberal-conservative lines of the U.S. cold war political continuum. By the year 2010, U.S. trade with Latin America will exceed trade with either Europe or the rim of Asia and the NAFTA region will be the world's most powerful economic engine. Since 1830 the Western Hemisphere has been the world's largest block of independent democracies, however flawed.

Latin America has now come to terms with the requisite institutionalization required to sustain a modern political democracy, and with the capitalization and distributional aspects of a modern free market economy. Their armed forces, much maligned in the analytical literature, are performing at a level of excellence both at home and within the international peacekeeping system that serves as a world model for Africa, Eastern Europe, Asia, and the Middle East. The view from this corner then is that the guarded optimists have the edge, and Latin America is the world's exciting and humane theater for the twenty-first century. An emerging literature seems to support that conclusion.

The reviewer is beholden to Editor John W. Madigan of *Parameters* for the opportunity to write the cited piece and several subsequent review essays on the strategic literature about Latin America.

NOTES

1. Russell W. Ramsey, "Strategic Reading on Latin America," *Parameters* 24:2 (Summer, 1994), pp. 133-6.
2. Robert A. Packenham, *The Dependency Movement: Scholarship and Politics in Development Studies* (Cambridge, Mass.: Harvard University Press, 1992).
3. Crisobal Kay, "Review," *Journal of Latin American Studies* 26: (May 1994): 513-15.
4. Robert S. Leiken, ed., *A New Moment in the Americas* (New Brunswick, N.J.: Transaction Publishers, 1994).
5. William W. Finan, ed., "Mexico," *Current History* 92 (February 1993); "Latin America," *Current History* 92: (March 1993): 572 "Latin America," *Current History* 93: (March 1994): 581; "Latin America," *Current History* 94: (February 1995): 589; and "North America," *Current History* 94: (March 1995): 590.
6. Pierre Etienne Dostert, *Latin America, 1994*, 29th ed., The World Today Series (Harper's Ferry, W. Va.: Stryker-Post Publications, 1995).
7. Eliana Cardosa and Ann Helwege, *Latin America's Economy* (Cambridge, Mass.: The M.I.T. Press, 1995).
8. Paul W. Drake, ed., *Money Doctors, Foreign Debts, and Economic Reforms in Latin America from the 1890s to the Present*, The Jaguar Series (Wilmington, Delaware: Scholarly Resources, 1994).
9. William C. Smith, Carlos H. Acuna, and Eduardo Gamarra. *Latin American Political Economy in an Age of Neoliberal Reform* (New Brunswick, N.J.: Transaction Press, 1994).
10. Jaime Suchlicki, ed., *North-South, the Magazine of the Americas* (October-November 1993, the "ABCs" issue); (November-December 1994, the "Summit of the Americas" issue).
11. Michale Radu, and Vladimir Tismaneanu, *Latin American Revolutionaries: Groups, Goals, and Methods* (Washington, D.C.: Pergamon Brrassey Press, 1990).
12. Timothy P. Wickham-Crowley, *Guerrillas and Revolution in Latin America: A Comparative Study of Insurgents and Regimes Since 1956* (Princeton, NJ: Princeton University Press, 1992).
13. Frederick M. Nunn, *The Time of the Generals: Latin American Professional Militarism in World Perspective* (Lincoln, Nev.: University of Nebraska Press, 1992).
14. David Pion-Berlin, "The Armed Forces in Politics: Gains and Snares in Recent Scholarship," *Latin American Research Review* 30 (Spring 1995): 147-62.

15. William Perry, and Max Primorac, "The Inter-American Security Agenda," *Journal of Inter-American Studies and World Affairs* 36 (Spring 1994): 111-27.

16. Russell W. Ramsey, "The Role of the Latin American Armed Forces in the 1990s," *Strategic Review* 20 (November-December 1992): 48-56.

17. Brian Loveman, "'Protected Democracies' and Military Guardianship: Political Transitions in Latin America, 1978-1993," *Journal of Inter-American Studies and World Affairs* 36 (Spring 1994): 105-89.

18. Lars Schoultz, William C. Smith, and Augusto Varas, eds., *Security, Democracy, and Development in U.S.-Latin American Relations* (New Brunswick, N.J.: Transaction Press, 1994).

19. Abraham F. Lowenthal, and Gregory F. Treverton, *Latin America in a New World* (Boulder, Colo.: Westview Press, 1994).

20. Robert A. Pastor, *Whirlpool: U.S. Foreign Policy Toward Latin America and the Caribbean* (Princeton, N.J.: Princeton University Press, 1992).

21. Martha L. Cottam, *Images and Intervention: U.S. Policies in Latin America* (Pittsburgh, Penn.: University of Pittsburgh Press, 1994).

22. L. Erik Kjonnerod, ed., *Evolving U.S. Strategy for Latin America and the Caribbean* (Washington, D.C.: National Defense University Press, 1992).

23. Russell W. Ramsey, "U.S. Strategy for Latin America," *Parameters* 24 (Autumn 1994): 70-83.

Strategic Review
Spring 1998

SHARING THE SECRETS: Open Intelligence and the War on Drugs

By J.F. Holden-Rhodes
Westport, CT: Praeger
1997. 235 pages. $55.00

DRUGS AND SECURITY IN THE CARIBBEAN: Sovereignty Under Siege

By Ivelaw Lloyd Griffith
University Park, PA: Pennsylvania State University Press
1997. 295 pages. $35.00 ($16.95 paperback)

Reviewed by Russell W. Ramsey

Two excellent current books on the Western Hemisphere drug war open possibilities for viewing the phenomenon differently, and consequently for deriving a more effective counter-narcotics strategy both in the United States and in the Latin American countries affected by the narcotics plague.

Sharing the Secrets gives the initial impression of being an argumentative plea for vindicating the author's intelligence gathering concept. Arthur J. R. Holden-Rhodes was a U.S. Marine Corps combat intelligence officer, and later a U.S. Army intelligence analyst working on drug war issues in U.S. Southern Command. Now pursuing a second career as an academician, he makes the case for the use of "open source intelligence" (OSINT), as opposed to the traditionally compartmentalized and classified intelligence program, on matters relating to the Drug War.

Drugs and Security in the Caribbean is the first comprehensive survey of the drug war in that sub-region of Latin America. Author Ivelaw Lloyd Griffith is political science professor at Florida International University (Miami), and is arguably the most authoritative and certainly the most comprehensively published scholar on Caribbean regional security issues. He grew up in Guyana.

Holden-Rhodes traces the history of U.S. Cold War strategic intelligence from its architects George S. Pettee and Sherman Kent, to the post-Cold War thinking of Joseph Markowitz. Holden-Rhodes believes that OSINT, in contrast to closeted and classified intelligence gathering and processing, draws a broader community of interests into the drug war. OSINT reduced parochialism within the intelligence community and its accompanying tunnel

Russell W. Ramsey is Distinguished Resident Professor at the U.S. Army School of the Americas, Ft. Benning, Georgia, and Professor of National Security Studies at Troy State University.

vision, and instead focuses upon home and hearth issues like personal safety and the cost of government. Thus, while OSINT broadens the base of domestic support for the drug war, it is nevertheless "an art that is best practiced by that small group of people who have the gift of discerning substance and direction from information that other simply offer up in shopping list form."

Holden-Rhodes then traces the development of counter-drug intelligence efforts, leading to the founding of the National Drug Intelligence Center at Johnstown, Pennsylvania in 1988. He concludes that drug intelligence products have never been employed correctly because intelligence production has been functionally linked to the discovery of short-term interdiction targets. This discussion flows into the quest for a counter-drug strategy. Failing to unshackle counter-drug strategy from national security strategy has crippled the effort, he shows. Holden-Rhodes argues that this structural error dates from 1973, when President Richard Nixon put his quest for a drug war strategy into the hands of the Watergate "plumbers": Egil Krogh, Gordon Liddy, E. Howard Hunt, and John Erlichman. The growing drug industry in Colombia is the base for Holden-Rhodes' analysis of an essentially flawed search to define the "drug threat," and his subsequent chapter on militarizing the war on drugs portrays a well-intentioned effort derailed by a distorted intelligence process that operates on the Cold War national security model. His chart linking military responses to identified narcotics syndicate threats would improve any textbook surveying U.S. national security policy.

Holden-Rhodes' description of the drug interdiction effort at the U.S. border with Mexico should be read in conjunction with Timothy J. Dunn's *The Militarization of the U.S.-Mexico Border, 1978-1992* (University of Texas at Austin, 1995). While both are critical of U.S. strategy, Holden-Rhodes blames flawed intelligence perception, while Dunn blames racist, imperialist prejudices in the national security community. Holden-Rhodes' last chapter, "Getting It Right," should have been made into two chapters, one containing his superb country-by-country analysis of the Western Hemisphere narco-industry threat, and one showing how his plan for employing OSINT would strengthen the U.S. national anti-drug effort.

In a candid portrayal of U.S. drug czar Barry McCaffrey, the highly decorated retired general who was Commander-in-Chief, U.S. Southern Command from 1994 to 1996, Holden-Rhodes believes that McCaffrey's forceful personality and high integrity will unite the U.S. national security community to wage the drug war, something the first three czars failed to do.

The Archbishop Colloredo desired sacred music of a certain style at Salzburg and in 1777 sacked Wolfgang Amadeus Mozart, the composer whose music most nearly touched the heavens, for failing to produce the desired product. The archbishops of intelligence at the CIA, DIA, DEA, NSA, and DEA may not even hire J. R. Holden-Rhodes. Indeed, his final chapter barely touches upon the ways that his OSINT concept could be used to alter an essentially fragmented and reactive U.S. anti-drug strategy. Yet his music touches the heavens in the sense that OSINT, applied at a coordinated national level, might become the vehicle to awaken the body politic to the fact that the drug war is both real and devastating, and that rationally based interdiction measures could achieve success.

In my article "Reading Up on the Drug War," *Parameters* (Fall 1995), I lamented the absence of serious strategic literature about the drug war. That complaint is now inoperative. Ivelaw Lloyd Griffith's *Drugs and Security in the Caribbean* is a meticulous description of the phenomenon, written in the precise idiom of national security calculus. Professors teaching courses that in any way touch upon the narcotics plague would do well to prescribe Griffith's first chapter for student reading. Griffith covers the waterfront by relating hallucinogenic drug use to politics, economics, geography, the natural environment, national security, and finally to sovereignty. His chart called "Conflict Interactions in the Geonarcotics Milieu" is a sophisticated contribution to scholarship, supported structurally by another chart called "Geonarcotics, a Framework."

Griffith relates the demand side to the supply side by sketching geographic locales and human motivations for narcotics consumption. The portraits are highly credible, and they close the door on the usual criticism about books on the drug war which portray supply side or demand side without showing the connection. The next section mixes data with humanistic anecdotes on how drugs are actually transported through the Caribbean regional security systems. And these are followed by a highly readable explanation of how the narcotics trade distorts economic flow and especially economic development in the Caribbean region.

In a chapter called "Crime, Justice, and Public Order," author Griffith shows the weakness of emerging criminal justice systems to cope with the narcotics plague, yet he also warns against the dangers of militarizing the effort. He opines that the Caribbean might be at "the dawn of Colombianization," a reference to the universally corrupting influence of narcotics abuse pitted against criminal justice systems. Griffith's final section on counter-measures in the Caribbean region reveals a better balance between supply side and demand side issues than is normally seen in books on this melancholy topic. His inventory of agencies and groups involved in the narcotics war is comprehensive and renders previous books on the Caribbean drug war obsolete. Declining to prescribe a unitary solution, he invites the people and leaders of the Caribbean region to "a long war" that must be waged on a "highly cooperative" basis.

Griffith's book has already been nominated for three awards: the Gordon K. Lewis Prize in Caribbean politics, the Bryce Wood Award in Latin American studies, and the Woodrow Wilson Foundation Award in social sciences analysis. This book may win or lose as a literary endeavor in three categories, but the reader can only win, for this is the best regional treatment of the narcotics plague yet written.

What can the Western Hemisphere gain from these works by Holden-Rhodes and Griffith? First, Holden-Rhodes offers a perceptual process by which to understand who and what is the enemy, and how best to employ society's resources against targets better selected. He does not want to discard existing intelligence mechanisms, but wishes to add his OSINT concept as the interpretive lens through which the American public and its elected leaders would view the drug war. Second, Griffith offers a precise regional portrait of the problem, emphasizing both supply side and demand side in prose that invites the reader to turn pages. Because he summarizes the threats presented by the Caribbean drug war in strategic terms as well as social impacts that ordinary citizens can visualize, his book tends to build support for solutions instead of frustrating or infuriating the reader. Third, both authors offer a model of excellent scholarship badly needed in a field which has often produced sloppily researched works portraying "great problems" with "no solutions."

Here are two views of the Western Hemisphere drug war, written in terms that national security planners and strategists can respect. Holden-Rhodes' OSINT concept may broaden the base of public support through a better understanding of the narcotics threat. Griffith meticulously links military and law enforcement threats to the quality of daily life in a region where millions of Americans work and take their vacations.

I recall when the spate of "what to do about guerrilla warfare" books in the 1960s clearly suggested that there was a neat solution attainable through the application of low intensity armed force and economic assistance. This giddy simplicity led to the quagmire in Vietnam, with shallow roots in public support. Holden-Rhodes and Griffith offer a way for the United States not to have a "narco-Vietnam" by gaining a truer understanding of the narcotics threat.

Both books would serve well as course texts, and both have already appeared on important desks within the Washington, DC beltway. To those who despair of rational solutions to the drug war, here, at least, are two intellectually strong gateways.

MILITARY REVIEW
Latin American Military Affairs
March-April 1996
RUSSELL W. RAMSEY

"During the Cold War, military professionals had difficulty finding accurate geostrategic Latin America reference works. Since the late 1830s, diplomats and military analysis have often relied on the British *Statesman's Yearbook*, a unique but sometimes inaccurate reference tool for Latin Americanists. Now, with democratization and privatization occupying national security and military analysis' attention, there is a fine new crop of reference literature available."

South America, Central America and the Caribbean: 1995. This 5th edition of Europa Publications' *Regional Surveys of the World* series is the most comprehensive work of its kind ever done because it relates public and private data from all sectors to national security issues. The directory includes specific information on companies, government agencies and security forces for immediate use by professionals.

"**The Caribbean and Latin America**" by John Chipman in *The Military Balance, 1994-1995*. The International Institute of Strategic Studies produces this famous series known colloquially as "Brassey's Annuals." The annual *Military Balance* provides analysis on Latin America's greatly reduced and rapidly changing military institutions. For descriptive information on Latin America's military forces, Chipman's article in the 1995 edition is the best. Developed at the London International Institute of Strategic Studies, it contains both threat descriptions and force analysis.

Latin America 1995 by Pierre Etienne Dostert. This is the best one-volume regional description in the English language because of its balance, scope and inclusion of strategic issues. The earlier annual issues still read with authenticity since their 1967 origin. Part of Stryker-Post's unique *The World Today* series on the world's regions, this Latin America volume integrates economic, political and military trends and gives a menu for deeper reading.

"**The Caribbean,**" "**Central America**" and "**South America**" by Claude C. Sturgill in *The Military History of the Third World Since 1945: A Reference Guide*. Sturgill's three Latin America chapters in this book are the best work available on US security assistance linkage with the region's military institutions. This is especially true because US security assistance programs to Latin America averaged 2 percent across the Cold War era, yet these programs are regularly villainized by leftist writers as the cause of regional lapses in military professionalism. Sturgill's book restores the balance and objectivity.

The Jaguar Series, Scholarly Resources Press. This series, edited by William H. Beezley and Colin M. MacLachlan, offers a strong entry to Latin American studies. Two excellent series entries are:

- *Rank and Privilege: The Military and Society in Latin America*. Edited by Linda Alexander Rodriguez. These essays fill the vacuum on the answers to such questions as how the great *caudillos* (strongmen) gave way to professional military officers in the 20th century and where the Latin American military officer's cultural ethos came from. The annotated bibliography is the best short piece of its kind in print. The book's introduction should be standard reading for Latin America regional students.
- *Money Doctors, Foreign Debts and Economic Reforms in Latin America from the 1890s to the Present*. Edited by Paul W. Drake. This Jaguar Series offering is a strong volume on the economic dimensions of emerging regional security. It shows how economic investment in the recent past often produced runaway deficit, destabilization and few new jobs. The mistakes are carefully analyzed.
- **Democracy in Latin America:** *Patterns and Cycles*. Edited by Roderic A. Camp. Here is the Jaguar Series 1996 offering on emerging democratic systems. While the military chapter is somewhat dated, the cultural-economic lin• *Democracy in Latin America* kage is blue chip. Professosr Camp is an expert on Mexican military forces.

    The North-South Center Series, University of Miami, under the leadership of Ambler H. Moss Jr. The center has no single name for its recent books on security and economic issues in Latin America, but several of its recently edited titles form a topical series of great merit.
- *Security, Democracy and Development in U.S.-Latin American Relations*. Edited by Lars Schoultz. William C. Smith and Augusto Varas. This book the outcome of a 1993 North-South Center symposium, opens the door to a discussion long blocked by competing ideology among scholars. It examines Western Hemisphere defense in an era of booming democracy, developing neolilberal economics are urgent social needs.
- *Latin American Political Economy in the Age of Neo-liberal Reform: Theoretical and Comparative Perspectives for the 1900s*. Edited by William C. Smith, Carlos Acuna and Eduardo Gamarra. This is an excellent North-South Center entry in the economics of national security field. Unlike the Drake volume, it concentrates on current processes and offers thoughtful policy recommendations.

- *Drug Trafficking in the Americas*. Edited by Bruce M. Bagley and William O. Walker III. This 1994 volume on a persistent and melancholy topic is comprehensive. However, constant criticism of "US policy that militarizes the drug war" is unbalanced and partially dated in 1996.

"Hopeful Neo-liberals, Derailed Collectivists: Emerging Paradigms on Latin America" by Russell W. Ramsey in *Comparative Strategy, an International Journal*. This is my January 1996 effort to organize the emerging literature ideologically. Military professionals can do better work on Latin America now than in the past because the reference literature and the interpretations about military-related events are less polemical, more variegated and more factual. model of some validity, at least for other countries? The papers published in 1994 in Schulz's slim book are the outcome of a January 1992 symposium at the Strategic Studies Institute, US Army War College. "The Cuban Armed Forces in Transition," an essay by Phyllis Greene Walker, is a gem in military force analysis. The book also includes Schulz's own essay on recommended US policy toward Cuba.

Cuba in Transition: Options for U.S. Policy by Gillian Gunn. This 1993 book by Gunn, a Georgetown University professor, is the best full-length study of what is to be done about Cuba. Easily the top analyst of Cuban military operations in Africa during the 1980s. Gunn now offers an agenda of carrots and sticks by which to bring the Cuban people out of Castro's personal aura and into a more participatory form of government no longer functioning as a regional pariah state. An essay by Gunn also appears in the Schulz book, paired with an ideologically different essay on the same topic by Marc Falcoff.

Chronicle of Higher Education: An Essay by Robert B. Toplin. Much of Castro's support has always come from the US academic community. Professor Stanley J. Stein of Princeton University challenged the Conference on Latin American History in his December 1960 speech to recognize that "evolutionary methods" and "parliamentary government" would not work for Latin America (*Hispanic-American Historical Review*, August 1961). This reality finally made academic print when Professor Toplin lamented it in his 30 March 1994 essay "Many Latin Americanists Continue to Wear Ideological Blinders."

Modern Latin American Revolutions by Eric Selbin. The trend of the radical left is to be a part of the newly democratizing and privatizing political and economic mainstream that is the 1990s' Latin America. However, not all agree. In Selbin's 1993 book, socialist revolutions in Latin America are valid and necessary. Selbin concludes that the Nicarguan Sandinistas won their struggle, despite their loss in the 1990 election, and that the Peru and El Salvador leftists may yet prevail in some form as well.

Russell W. Ramsey, Ph.D., D.Min.

Guerrillas and Revolution in Latin America by Timothy P. Wickham-Crowley. In his 1992 book, Wickham-Crowley concludes that only the 1959 Cuban and the 1979 Sandinista revolutions in Nicaragua ever achieved legitimacy. He meticulously examines the armed leftist struggles within Latin American during the Cold War. He also shows how erroneous US support for *mafioso* regimes was the real cause of communist victory in Cuba and Nicaragua. He argues convincingly that such leftist efforts as Che Guevara's 1967 operation in Bolivia were idiosyncratic, not comprehensive, in public support. **MR**

Russell W. Ramsey is the distinguished resident professor, US Army School of the Americas, Fort Benning, Georgia and lectures in Spanish on strategy at the inter-American Defense College. Fort McNair, Washington, D.C. He received a B.S. from the US Military Academy, an M.A. from the University of Southern Mississippi and a Ph.D. from the University of Florida. He has served in a variety of military positions in Southeast Asia, Panama and the Continental United States, to include commander, parachute infantry company 1ˢᵗ Air Cavalry Division, Vietnam; counterinsurgency instructor, School of the Americas, Panama: mobilization designation Reservist desk officer, Office of the Joint Chiefs of Staff, J5, Strategy-Western Hemisphere. He is the author of Soldiers and Guerrillas, a history of modern rural violence in Colombia, and wrote the first counterinsurgency course curriculum for the School of the Americas when it was located in Panama.

About the Author

Russell W. Ramsey is the longest standing and most widely published U.S. scholar of the Latin American military scene. He was the pilot project officer at the U.S. Army School of the Americas in Panama (1960 – 1962) when (then) Attorney General Robert Kennedy installed the counter-insurgency program. As an Army Reserve officer, he was the Desk Officer for Long Range Strategy (J-5), U.S. Joint Chiefs of Staff in the 1980's. His doctoral dissertation on the Colombian Violencia (1946 – 1965), published in 1970, is still a best seller in Colombia today. He was Chief of Latin American Studies for the U.S. Air Force Command and Staff College from 1987 to 1992, and Distinguished Civilian Professor for the U.S. Army School of the Americas from 1992 to 2000. His publications appear in every major U.S. journal of strategic studies and of Latin American Studies. Currently he is professor of Latin American Studies at Troy State University, working to establish the advanced academic programs at the newly opened (January 2001) Western Hemisphere Institute for Security Cooperation (WHINSEC).

www.ingramcontent.com/pod-product-compliance
Lightning Source LLC
Chambersburg PA
CBHW051449280526
45785CB00003B/1496